DATING A WIDOWER

DATING A WIDOWER

ABEL KEOGH

Dating a Widower:
Starting a Relationship with a Man Who's Starting Over
Second Edition
Copyright © 2020 by Abel Keogh

Published by
Ben Lomond Press
All rights reserved
ISBN: 9781712156988

Cover design by Brian Halley
Cover design copyright © 2020 by Abel Keogh
Interior Design by NovelNinjutsu.com

This is a self-help book. Opinions expressed are those of the author.

TABLE
OF CONTENTS

INTRODUCTION
TO THE SECOND EDITION

I WROTE THE FIRST EDITION of *Dating a Widower* because I witnessed too many women getting hurt after starting serious relationships with widowers who weren't mentally or emotionally ready for commitment. While the first edition provided important guidance to thousands of women, there are subjects and topics that needed to be added. For example, social media was a new thing and didn't even receive a mention in the first edition. Since then, sites like Facebook and Instagram have become an integral part of most people's lives. As a result, this edition addresses questions like what to do with the late wife's Facebook page, and whether it's appropriate for widowers to post photos and memories of their late wives after they start dating.

This edition also provides insight into widower psychology so that you can better understand their thought processes and the reasons behind their words and actions.

Empowered with this knowledge, you can identify red flags and know if a widower is ready to open his heart to you or is simply looking for a placeholder while he grieves.

Finally, this edition teaches you how to set and maintain healthy boundaries with widowers. It's not easy to ask someone who's lost a spouse to put the past to the side and make you number one, but setting healthy boundaries is vital for your mental health and emotional wellbeing. It is a dependable way to know if widowers are serious about starting a new relationship.

Dating widowers comes with a host of unique challenges and issues you won't experience in other relationships. Whether you've just met or are in a long-term, serious relationship, this book helps you know where the widower is on his grief journey and if he's ready and willing to start a new chapter of his life. It also provides the guidance and clarity you need to asses and determine if dating a widower is right for you.

My wife, Julianna, and I wish that a resource like this book had been available when we were dating. It would have helped me understand my confusing and conflicting feelings and helped Julianna better navigate the unique issues she encountered. Our story, along with the experiences of many other women, are part of this book. It is my hope that these stories, along with all the supplemental information, will help you know if the widower you're dating is ready to open his heart and spend the rest of his life with you.

Abel Keogh
January 2020

1

WHY DO WIDOWERS DATE SOON AFTER THEIR LATE WIVES DIE?

A FEW MONTHS AFTER MY late wife, Krista, and I were married, we witnessed a widower make a pass at Krista's grandmother, Loretta. His wife had died a few days earlier, and her funeral was later that morning.

We were in the kitchen helping Loretta prepare some food for the lunch that was to follow the funeral. The recent widower knocked at the door, and Loretta answered. From the kitchen, Krista and I could hear every word they both said. Most of their conversation had to do with the funeral and lunch arrangements, but just as the widower was about to leave, he said to Loretta, "I'll be calling on you tomorrow."

I glanced over at Krista to confirm that I had heard correctly. The aghast look on Krista's face told me that I had. My mind was spinning as I tried to process his words.

1

This man hadn't even buried his wife, and he already had plans to ask Krista's grandmother out on a date. In my mind, the only kind of man who would even consider dating that quickly after his wife died was a man no longer in love. I was not acquainted with the widower or his late wife, but from what Loretta had told us, they had been married for over forty years. Loretta's husband had died twenty years earlier, and as far as I knew, she had never dated anyone after her husband passed away. Wasn't that what widows and widowers were supposed to do? Wasn't there a rule that they had to wait at least one year before dating again? I wasn't sure, but as I looked out the nearby window at the widower walking toward his home, whatever sympathy and compassion I felt for him earlier vanished.

Loretta returned to the kitchen, and without a word to either Krista or myself, continued her work.

Krista and I exchanged looks, both wondering if one of us should comment on what we overheard. After a few moments of silence between us, Krista spoke.

"Grandma, did he ask you out?" she asked.

"He alluded to something like that," Loretta chuckled.

"You're not going out with him, are you?" Krista said in a voice that made me think she was going to lose all respect for her grandmother if she even considered dating this man.

Loretta waved her hand dismissively and said that she had no interest in dating anyone.

Krista and I looked at each other again. I shrugged and returned to my work. I found it strange how casually

Loretta dismissed the entire incident. Questions swirled through my mind. Had she been asked out by this man while his wife was alive? Did it strike her as odd that he had asked her out just a few days after his wife died? Had she been asked out by enough widowers in the past that she was hardened to their advances?

I never asked any of those questions, but looking back, I wish I had. Maybe Loretta would have imparted some wisdom about her widowed neighbor that would have helped me understand his actions. Perhaps she had some insight on how widows and widowers grieve. At the very least, her words might have given me some comfort two years later, when I found myself with a strong desire to start dating only two months after Krista took her own life.

Losing a spouse is harder for men than it is for women.

Widowers are more likely than widows to experience declines in their physical and emotional health in the months and years following their wife's passing[1]. They're more likely to suffer from depression and chronic stress. Many widowers have difficulty sleeping and problems concentrating, and often show little or no interest in activities they enjoyed when their wife was alive. As a result, widowers are one-third more likely to die after being recently widowed. Widows, on the other hand, have no increased chance of dying after their husbands pass away.[2]

3

When a man's wife dies, he loses more than just a partner. He loses his confidant, his lover, his companion, and his biggest supporter. His identity as a protector, provider, and leader vanishes. With few reasons to get out of bed in the morning, widowers view the emptiness in their lives as a problem that needs to be solved. And how do they fix their broken lives and grieving hearts? They start dating again.

It's not a question of *if* widowers will date again, but how soon it will happen.

Over the years, I've spoken with and coached hundreds of widowers of various ages and backgrounds. Nearly every widower I've spoken with had a strong desire to date in the weeks or months after his wife's death. It didn't matter how long they were married, how their wife died, their cultural background, their beliefs, their values, or anything else. Nearly all of them described an urge to find companionship soon after their wife passed away. Some of them fought or brushed aside these feelings and waited several months or years before finally dating, but most of them were quick to act in the hope that being with another woman would alleviate their pain and loneliness.

If you're dating a widower, it's vital that you understand this internal need widowers have for companionship, because it's what drives them to date long before they're emotionally or mentally ready for a serious relationship. Most widowers—especially recent widowers—aren't looking for a serious relationship when they start dating again. What they're looking for is *companionship*.

Widowers who seek companionship want a woman to do one thing: fill the gaping hole in their hearts. They believe that by having someone—anyone—in their life, their hearts will be healed and the empty feeling that consumes them will vanish. This desire for companionship is so strong that widowers will start a serious relationship with women they wouldn't date if they weren't grieving.

Let me give you a personal example. In the months following Krista's death, I started a relationship with a woman I'll call Jennifer—a female friend who lived six hundred miles away in Phoenix, Arizona. Though Jennifer and I had been friends for many years, we had never dated or been romantically involved with each other prior to Krista's passing. Our relationship started innocently enough when Jennifer periodically called to check up on me after Krista died. She'd ask how I was doing, and we'd spend five or ten minutes catching up. Somewhere along the way, our conversations become more serious, and our friendship evolved into a long-distance relationship.

After a few months of talking on the phone every night and monthly flights to see each other in person, Jennifer believed we would get married and live happily ever after. Though I never dissuaded Jennifer from drawing that conclusion, marrying her was something I could never personally see happening. Her dreams of the two of us spending the rest of our lives together came to an abrupt end when I dumped her after becoming serious with Julianna. (More details about this long-distance relationship are found in my memoir *Room for Two*).

Under normal circumstances, I never would have dated Jennifer or become involved in a serious relationship with her, because we simply weren't compatible. However, because I craved companionship and was looking for someone—anyone—to help fill the void Krista left in my heart, I ignored obvious red flags, brushed aside my internal doubts, and let the relationship become serious. It was only when I realized that there was someone who matched up perfectly with me—someone I could see myself spending the rest of my life with—that the relationship with Jennifer came to an end.

I share this story to illustrate the fact that widowers often start dating for the wrong reasons. Relationships that begin because widowers want to heal their broken hearts or fill the void in their lives never end well. And you don't have to take my word for it. Throughout this book, you'll read heartbreaking stories of women who were in relationships with widowers who could never make these women feel like the most important person in their lives.

By now, some of you are wondering if the widower you're dating is serious about your relationship or is simply using you as a placeholder until someone better comes along. In the upcoming chapters, I'll show how you can know if the widower you're dating is using you to soothe his broken heart or is actually ready to start a new chapter of his life with you. The purpose of this chapter is to help you understand the motivations and desires that nudge widowers back into the dating game before they're emotionally ready to take that step. When you know that widowers are driven by an internal need to find companionship, it's easier to evaluate their words, actions, and behavior.

At the beginning of this chapter, I told a story about a widower who announced his interest in dating Krista's grandmother on the day of his late wife's funeral. Today, I look back on this widower's actions with a lot more clarity and charity. Though I still think he should have waited until *after* the funeral to ask Loretta out, I better understand the reason behind his actions and regret judging him as harshly as I did. I don't know if that widower ever dated anyone or found love again. If he did remarry, I hope he could give her his whole heart and soul. Loretta, on the other hand, never went out with him or anyone else for the rest of her life. She passed away in 2005, four years after Krista died.

ERIN'S STORY

I started dating my widower not even four months after he lost his late wife due to complications from cystic fibrosis. From the beginning, there were the typical issues surrounding dating a widower: pictures of her all over the house, her belongings still in the closets and drawers, drama with his former in-laws being upset that he had started dating so quickly after her death, etc. My initial reaction was to end the relationship before it even began, but I felt a strong connection to him and was hopeful that things would improve as time went on.

Little did I know that one year later, despite our recent engagement and the fact that we were living together, the issues surrounding his being a widower would be just as difficult as they were on day one. It didn't matter that her things were removed from the house and that her family was no longer in contact with him. Her presence was everywhere. To make matters worse, we were living in the same house he'd lived in with her, but he had a job transfer coming soon, so we would be moving to another state. I was hopeful that once we were married and living somewhere else, we could begin our future together, minus the ghost. However, almost every discussion surrounding our wedding and impending move ended with one of us yelling, and the other in tears.

I was terrified that my entire life was going to be spent living in her shadow, feeling like I was never quite good enough. It became obvious to me that my widower had never fully mourned his late wife. I began to notice situations in our day-to-day lives where he found it easier to sweep his feelings under the rug rather than risk upsetting me by speaking up. Also, when talking to outsiders, he'd pretend like that period of his life didn't happen, that he'd been single right up until we met. I wondered if he'd ever find a way to move past his grief and begin his future with me. I suggested he see a therapist, or that we attend couples' therapy, but he wanted no part of it.

Unfortunately for me, his grief came to a head five weeks before our wedding and resulted in him calling the entire thing off. I found out weeks later that he was telling people he ended it because I wasn't able to accept the fact that he was married before! In the end, my ex took zero responsibility for his actions and refused to see that his past was standing in the way of his future with me, or anything else. Moving forward was one of the hardest things I've ever had to do, but looking back, he did me the biggest favor of my life by walking away.

I'm now about to marry someone who makes me feel like the center of his world, twenty-four seven. I only hope my ex has gotten the help that he needed, and I truly wish him nothing but the best. My advice to those out there dealing with similar circumstances? Follow your gut. If you feel like you're second, it's probably because you are.

PEGGY'S STORY

The man I am dating is a widower. I knew him and his wife before she died. I liked them both and thought they were a great couple. I was divorced by the time we all met.

A few months ago, his wife was killed in a tragic accident. I thought about him and wondered how he and his children were getting along. Suddenly, he was thrown into the role of caretaker of children, house, animals, carpools, appointments, dance practice, and kid scheduling and management, in addition to the already full-time position of sole financial provider. I was exhausted thinking about it.

Then he called me. We shared a glass of wine and became good friends. He has handled the transition into his new life with realistic expectations. He has been forthcoming about his wife, his children, his relationship with me, and what the community thinks about us as a couple. I am not offended when he tells stories about his wife. That would be absurd on my part. She was his main companion for more than 20 years. No one expects him to erase her from his memory.

He has not made her into a saint. She was a real person with real qualities and imperfections. I am different enough from her that he has not compared us in any way. I don't feel like I'm expected to replace her. He doesn't need someone to do household chores.

A man needs someone to talk to and laugh with, someone who cares about him and is relieved when they receive a text saying his flight landed safely. Everyone wants to know that someone cares about them.

His teenage children live at home with him. He has had frank conversations about going on without their mother. He assured them that while he will never stop loving her, it would be unrealistic to think he would live his life alone and sad.

The kids know me as a mom from school, but they had a mother, and she did a great job raising them with her limited time. They are well-rounded kids and will do well, in part due to her influence on them, but also because of the way their dad has modeled how to handle grief and loss. He has shown them that life is for the living, and they should continue to do just that.

The *right* amount of time to grieve is different for everyone, and at some point, a person just needs to be allowed to be happy again. I have learned a lot about grief after tragedy from him.

I doubt very much that either of us would have chosen the paths our lives have taken, but the result is that we are together. This has been very good for me, and it seems to be good for him, too.

Experience is not what happens to a man. It's what a man does with what happens to him. Becoming a widower is something that happened to him. But he has not let it define him as a man.

2

WIDOWER PSYCHOLOGY 101

MOST PEOPLE'S UNDERSTANDING OF HOW widowers grieve, when they should date again, and how women should treat widowers is formed by books, movies, and television shows. These pop-culture widowers are generally portrayed as "broken" and "lost" and men who just need the right woman to come along and "fix" them. In these same stories, the woman who manages to mend their widower's heart is pretty, charming, understanding, and patient, and always manages to say the right things at just the right time.

At some point in the story, the widower breaks up with this nearly perfect woman, only to realize that he made a horrible mistake. In order to win her back, he instantly sets aside his grief and makes some dramatic show of his love before this woman's heart is lost to him forever. If the widower has children, they're usually the first to realize Dad is missing out on a great opportunity and come up with ingenious ways to help him reunite with this woman. By the end of the story, the widower and this new love end up together and live happily ever after.

While these pop culture depictions of widowers make for good page-turners or binge-watching sessions on Netflix, they're detached from reality. If you really want to understand why widowers act and behave the way they do, you need to have a paradigm shift in the way you perceive them. Instead of viewing widowers as "broken" and needing "fixing," you need to see them as they really are: men.

That's right—widowers are men. It doesn't matter how long they were married, how their wives passed away, or how long it's been since their wives died—*widowers act, think, and grieve like men.* When you learn how men grieve and how losing their wives influences their thoughts, words, and actions, it becomes much easier to understand and interpret their behavior.

In this chapter, you'll learn the four foundational principles of widower psychology. Armed with this knowledge, you'll be able to understand the reasons behind a widower's words and actions. In addition, this information will help you better discern if the widower you're dating is actually ready to open his heart to you or is just looking for a placeholder until someone better comes along.

PRINCIPLE #1: MEN EXPRESS THEIR TRUE FEELINGS THROUGH ACTIONS—NOT WORDS

In books or movies, widowers usually make a dramatic speech to show the audience, and the woman whose heart he's trying to win, that he's really in love with her. This speech gushes with so much emotion that there's no doubt in anyone's mind that the widower is finally ready to open his heart again. In the real world, words from widowers are cheap and mean nothing. If you want to know how a widower really feels about you, watch his actions instead of listening to his words.

In coaching sessions, one of the most common subjects that comes up is the inconsistency between widowers' words and actions. For example, a widower tells the woman he's dating that he's in love with her and can see a long and happy future together. Despite these wonderful, affectionate words, this same widower doesn't remove his wedding band, keeps his late wife's clothes in the closet, and refuses to tell close friends and family about the new woman he's seeing.

What accounts for this discrepancy?

In Chapter 1, you learned about the strong internal desire widowers have for companionship. This longing drives widowers to date before they're emotionally or mentally ready for a serious relationship. As a result, widowers will say that they love you, but inside, they're still sorting out conflicting feelings of love, loss, hope, grief, and guilt. They'll tell you that they see a future with you when, in reality, they don't know how much longer the relationship will last. They'll promise you the moon in order to keep the relationship going because the last thing they want is to be alone. While their loving and promising words may be what you want to hear, it's their actions that show how widowers really feel about you and the relationship.

Widowers who are ready to open their hearts will *show* that they love you. They'll remove their wedding rings, take down the shrines, scatter her ashes, pack up her belongings, update their relationship status on social media, and introduce you to friends and family. Most importantly, they'll figure out a way to work through their grief so they can fully open their heart to you. Widowers who can't back up their words with actions know deep inside that they're not ready for a serious, committed relationship.

Let me give you a personal example: When I was in a long-distance relationship with Jennifer, I told her over and over that I loved her and hinted that I wanted to spend the rest of my life with her. However, my actions never backed up any of my words. Photos of Krista covered the walls of my home. I never considered removing the gold wedding band I wore on a chain around my neck. I kept my relationship with Jennifer a secret from family and friends for as long as possible. Each morning, I got up early and went for long, marathon-training runs with Julianna. In short, my actions and words never aligned. If I was truly in love with Jennifer, I would have taken down the photos, removed the wedding band, and told everyone I knew about her. And I wouldn't have spent every morning accompanying Julianna on her runs.

If Jennifer had paid attention to my actions instead of my words, odds are the relationship never would have become as serious as it did. But since I kept telling Jennifer the things she wanted to hear, our relationship continued until I unceremoniously dumped her a few months after we became serious. (You can read more about our relationship in my memoir *Room for Two*.)

Conversely, when Julianna and I were together, I backed up my words with actions. I removed my wedding ring, packed up the photos of Krista, introduced Julianna to friends and family, and even agreed to sell my recently remodeled home so the two of us could start our married life in a new town. Instead of just telling Julianna I loved her (which I often said), I did everything possible to show her I was ready to open my heart and start a new chapter of my life with her.

Some women spend years waiting for widowers to scatter their late wives' ashes, make their homes into places where the women can feel comfortable, or invite them to family dinners and activities. Despite their girlfriends' patience and understanding, the widowers always come up with an excuse or justification as to why nothing's changed. They can't back up their words with actions because deep inside, they know they're not ready to fully commit. Companionship is good enough for them.

A widower who is truly ready to open his heart won't make excuses. Instead, he will slay dragons, climb mountains, and swim oceans to show his love for you. He will figure out the best and fastest way to overcome his grief and make you the number one person in his heart and mind. While there may be the occasional speedbump or setback along the way, you will see him making sacrifices to move your relationship forward. There is one exception to this principle (see Principle #4), but in general, paying attention to a widower's actions is the best way to know if he really loves you and how invested he is in the relationship.

If you're dating a widower who's all talk but no action, end the relationship. You deserve someone who will treat you like a queen instead of a placeholder. You deserve to be the primary person in his heart.

PRINCIPLE #2: MEN MUST HEAL THEMSELVES

In the movie *Sleepless in Seattle*, the character Sam (Tom Hanks) pours out his heart on a national radio show. Toward the end of their conversation, the show's host asks Sam if he could love anyone as much as he loved his wife.

Sam: Well, that's hard to imagine.

Host: What are you going to do?

Sam: Well, I'm going to get out of bed every morning and breathe in and out all day. And after a while, I won't have to remind myself to do it. And then after a while, I won't remember how perfect things were.

Host: Sam, tell me what was so special about your wife.

Sam: It was a million tiny little things, and when you added them up, it meant we were supposed to be together. And I knew it—I knew it the very first time I touched her. It was like coming home, only to no home I'd ever known. I was just taking her hand to help her out of a car. And I knew it. It was ... like magic.

How do women react to Sam's words of love and sadness about his late wife? Relationship columnist Emily Yoffe describes it perfectly in an essay she wrote for *The New York Times*:

> But what really makes the widower today's perfect mate? The key is in the crucial scene in which Annie Reed, played by Meg Ryan, hears widower Hanks on a radio call-in show talking about how much he loved his wife. At that moment she, thousands of other listeners and every woman in the audience falls madly in love with him. It is an odd thing to fall in love with someone because he loves someone else. But his pain is at the heart of his appeal—because the fantasy forces you to conclude that only you can heal it.[3]

This pop culture illusion has caused many women to start serious relationships with widowers—even when they think the widower isn't ready for one—and stay in them long past the relationship's expiration date. They think that if they're patient enough, or say or do the right thing, the widower's heart will mend.

Grief, however, is a solitary journey. There's nothing *you* can do to help widowers heal their hearts. There are no magic words, no acts of love or service, or anything you can change about yourself that will help a widower overcome his grief. The only person who can heal his pain is the widower himself.

A widower will take down his late wife's photos when he *wants* you to feel comfortable in his home. He will stop frequenting the cemetery when he *wants* to focus on the living. He will stop talking about the late wife when he *wants* to talk about you and your interests. He will introduce you to close friends and family members when he *wants* you to meet them. He will heal and open his heart when he *wants* to spend the rest of his life with you. All you can do is be your real, authentic self. That alone should be reason enough for a widower to want to move forward.

When I was dating Jennifer, I could never fully open my heart to her because I knew the relationship wasn't right. Even though Jennifer had many qualities that I loved and admired and we were compatible in several key areas, I was never motivated to actually do anything that would show my love for her. I rationalized my inaction by telling myself I was still grieving. I thought my muddled feelings would eventually sort themselves out as I worked through my grief. Instead, my feelings only grew more conflicted and confused the longer the relationship went on.

With Julianna, it was the exact opposite. From our very first date, I knew there was something special about her. I realized that to have any chance of the two of us spending the rest of our lives together, I had to show her that I was ready to move forward. When I took off my wedding band, it was because I *wanted* to show her that I wasn't going to let a symbol of my past marriage come between us. When I took down the photos of Krista, it was because I *wanted* Julianna to feel comfortable and spend lots of time in my home. When I decided to sell my house so Julianna and I could start our married life together elsewhere, it was because I *wanted* our marriage to have the best chance of success. I did all this and more because I *wanted* to spend the rest of my life with Julianna.

Julianna never tried to heal my grief or mend my heart. She knew that was something I had to do. All she did was be her wonderful self. Spending the rest of my life with such an amazing woman was the only motivation I needed to move forward.

I've talked with many women who have been in widower relationships that dragged on for years because they mistakenly thought that if they were more patient, caring, or understanding, the widowers would eventually come to their senses. The truth is that if a widower can't make you the primary person in his heart within the first year of the relationship, it's never going to happen. Investing any more time past a year is simply a waste.

For those who are wondering how my relationship with Jennifer would have turned out if I had never met Julianna, it would have eventually ended. It probably would have dragged on for another six months or so, but sooner or later, Jennifer would have lost patience waiting for me to get my act together, or I would have grown tired of a relationship that wasn't going anywhere. There is *nothing* Jennifer could have said or done that would have made me fully open my heart to her.

If you're dating a widower who can't move on, please don't feel like you said or did something wrong or that you weren't patient enough. There's nothing you can do to save a relationship with a widower who's in a relationship for the wrong reasons. The best thing you can do for yourself is to end the relationship. Staying in such a relationship will result in more self-doubt, anxiety, and misery. You deserve someone who can give you his heart and full attention. If the widower can't do that, it's time to find someone else who can.

PRINCIPLE #3: WIDOWERS CAN ACTIVELY LOVE ONE WOMAN AT A TIME

Women typically want to feel secure in romantic relationships. That's one reason why women don't get serious with a divorced man who's still angry and bitter toward his ex-wife or a single man who's still anguishing over a failed romance. They know these men haven't fully moved on from past relationships and understand that getting involved in something serious will result in a constant battle for the man's heart, mind, and attention.

When it comes to widowers, however, these concerns are often set aside. Reasons for this include the belief that the widower wouldn't be dating if he wasn't ready for a relationship, or thinking that they can somehow heal the widower's heart, or simply not knowing the issues that come with dating a man who's lost his wife. The truth is, it doesn't matter if a man is single, divorced, or widowed. If he can't give you the lion's share of his heart, the relationship will never work.

While the human heart has a great capacity for love, men can only actively love one woman at a time. The keyword here is "actively." Widowers will always love their late wives, and there's nothing wrong with that. I still love Krista. Men, however, can only devote their thoughts, feelings, and attentions to one woman at a time. That means to have successful relationships, widowers need to focus their time, energy, and attention on building and strengthening a new relationship instead of mourning and pining after their late wives. When widowers can't do this, the women they're dating feel like a third wheel. Many of the women I coach say it feels like they're competing with a ghost. While it's unrealistic to expect a widower to stop loving his late wife, it's acceptable for you to expect to feel like you're the most important person in his heart and that 99.9% of his thoughts and energy are focused on you.

For example, when Jennifer and I were together, my thoughts were usually on Krista and how much I missed her. No matter how much time Jennifer and I spent together or how much fun we had, I found myself constantly wondering if Krista would like this activity, what we'd be doing if she was still alive, or what she thought about my dating so soon after her death. As hard as I tried, I could never fully focus my thoughts and feelings on Jennifer. Everything, it seemed, came back to Krista.

Conversely, Julianna was always at the top of my mind. When we were together, my thoughts were focused on her welfare and happiness. When we were apart, I counted down the minutes until we could be together again. I awoke before 5:00 a.m. and drove to her apartment every morning to go on long training runs with her because it meant I could spend an extra hour with her before work. I constantly thought about a future with her and imagined my life with her by my side—not just as a girlfriend, but as a wife and eventual mother to any kids we might have. That's something I never envisioned with Jennifer.

This doesn't mean that I stopped thinking about Krista or my loss. In fact, thoughts and feelings about Krista were still present and bubbled to the surface on occasion. When they arose, I put them in a special place in my heart and dealt with them at a more appropriate time. Occasionally, there were bumps and setbacks that made Julianna wonder if I really was ready to start a new life with her. Each day, however, I gave her a bigger and bigger piece of my heart, until 99% of it was dedicated to her.

If you feel like a third wheel in your widower relationship, it's because the widower's heart still belongs to his late wife. This doesn't mean the relationship is hopeless, but as we discussed in the previous section, opening his heart is something only the widower can do, and it requires action on his part to show that he's making room for you.

Never stay in a relationship where you're constantly competing with a ghost. You'll never win. Instead, find a relationship where ghosts of the past don't haunt your present or future.

PRINCIPLE #4: WIDOWERS DON'T EQUATE SEX WITH COMMITMENT

Earlier in this chapter, I wrote that widowers express love through their actions. There is, however, one exception to this rule: sex. There's an entire chapter later in the book that discusses things you should consider before sleeping with a widower. The purpose of this section is to discuss how widowers think about and approach sex.

Men and women view sex differently. Women are generally more selective about who they sleep with. They also tend to equate sex with commitment—or at the very least, a way to up the commitment level in a relationship. Men, on the other hand, will sleep with just about anyone and tend to equate sex with pleasure. Sex means more to men if they love the person they're sleeping with, but unless they've already opened their heart to that woman, sex doesn't make them more emotionally or mentally invested in a relationship.

It's a common misconception to think that widowers associate sex with commitment because they were in monogamous relationships with their late wives. In reality, it doesn't matter how long they were married or if they were faithful to their late wives, because when they start dating again, they view sex just like any other single man.

Having sex—no matter how great the sex is or how often you have it—won't help a widower overcome his grief or open his heart. Unless he has feelings for the woman he's sleeping with, sex is just another way for a widower to dull the pain and grief he's experiencing. So, don't think that a great night in bed is going to revitalize a flagging relationship or make him fall in love with you.

When you decide to become intimate with a widower is ultimately up to you. Knowing how widowers think about and view sex, I suggest holding off on sexual intimacy at least until you're confident that he's actually ready for a serious, committed relationship. I've coached many women who felt emotionally devastated when their relationship ended and they realized the widower was simply using them for sex. Setting healthy boundaries about when you become intimate is a great way to filter out widowers who are simply looking for sexual fulfilment instead of a serious relationship. Many widowers will test the boundaries you set regarding intimacy, but widowers who are looking for a long-term relationship will, in the end, respect whatever line you draw. Widowers who are simply looking for someone to keep them warm at night will become angry, annoyed, or demanding when they're not getting the bedroom action they believe they're entitled to. Never give in to a widower's demand for sex or be guilted into becoming intimate before you're ready to take that step. Widowers who try to force you into bed don't deserve a second chance. The best thing you can do is dump them and never get back together with them.

Julianna had very clear boundaries about when she was going to become physically intimate. The last thing she wanted in our relationship was to be a replacement for Krista, and she wasn't going to have sex with me until she was confident that I was ready to make her number one. Those rules were laid out clearly and early in our relationship. I chose to respect her boundaries, and I am very glad I did. Waiting until we were both ready to take that step made sex more meaningful for both of us and helped cement our commitment to each other.

Specifics about sex and intimacy with widowers—including how to set boundaries, deal with widowers who feel guilty having sex, or what to do when the late wife is in the bedroom—can be found in Chapter 6. The point of this section is to raise awareness of how widowers think about sex so you can avoid feeling used by widowers who have no interest in you beyond the bedroom.

Understanding these four principles of widower psychology will help you put a widower's words and actions into context. When you do this, you'll be able to understand the motivation and reasons behind his actions and how serious he is about a long-term relationship.

One thing to keep in mind is that unless a widower has been in lots of different relationships since his late wife died, dating is a new experience for him, too. He probably doesn't fully understand why he's acting a certain way or the feelings that are bubbling up inside him.

Finally, just because a widower isn't ready for a serious relationship doesn't mean he can't change. In the coming chapters, I'll discuss more about setting healthy boundaries and how to know if a widower is capable of overcoming his grief and opening his heart. In the next chapter, we'll discuss red flags that are sure signs the widower isn't ready to love again.

ANN'S STORY

I hesitate to call our courtship and marriage a success, because I don't see love and long-term relationships in the black-and-white manner of women's magazines or dating self-help books. Success is relative, even if failure is painted with a universal brush.

When I asked my husband, Rob, why he thought we succeeded when other couples in our situation fail, he replied only half-jokingly, "It was my stellar personality." That's not quite true, but it's not entirely incorrect, either. Relationships that work depend on both partners wanting them to do so.

When we met, I had been widowed for 11 months. Rob's wife had died four months earlier. While I'd begun dating, he'd decided to wait to give himself time to recuperate from Shelley's death and the months he'd spent taking care of her.

We cultivated a "just friends" relationship, which began with meeting via an online widowed support board. Eventually we communicated more using email, IM, and the telephone.

Rob was the one who suggested elevating our friendship to dating. Before that, I was content despite knowing that our relationship was a bit flirtier than "just friends." However, I didn't try to analyze his actions or read between his words. Like any man, Rob said what he meant, and his actions spoke just as clearly. If a man is interested, he tells you, and if there is a potential long-term option, he acts.

Both of us being widowed probably made things easier. I didn't have to wonder how he felt, nor did I take anything related to his grief personally. Our relationship was a separate issue. Grief is not a *couple's* activity, and it's not an obstacle to moving on with someone else. The right person is more motivation than any widower needs to pack up the past and build a new life. If new love stirred up grief, it was acknowledged, and then we moved on. If he'd hemmed and hawed or had thrown up continual roadblocks in the form of his late wife, children, or in-laws, I would have known that he wasn't really serious about us.

How did I know?

I used those things to put off suitors who didn't interest me or with whom I saw no potential for a long-term relationship. It's easier than saying, "I'm not that into you."

Does grief come up? Yes, but only a little bit. If a widower loves you, grief won't derail what you have together. With time, patience, and shared effort, you can build a lasting relationship just like any couple does.

Rob made it clear that I was his priority. He was considerate of his daughters' conflicted reactions to us but did not let their grief dictate his decisions. He let family and friends know that he was a grown man who knew his own mind and heart. Not that we met with much active interference or criticism. Most people expressed support and genuine happiness for us.

Bottom line is that our actions set the tone for our children, family, and friends. We knew what we wanted and acted accordingly, and whatever issues came up were discussed and dealt with immediately—just like any other healthy relationship. Widowed people fall in love, and they do live happily ever after—again.

JENNIFER'S STORY

My relationship with my widower is one of three hearts. Without his late wife, our relationship wouldn't exist. We have been together for almost two-and-a-half years, but because of her, the building of our relationship started long before that.

His late wife became a friend of mine through our oldest sons. Our sons went to the same summer camp when they were in elementary school, and they wanted to spend time together after camp ended. My friendship with my widower's late wife was easy. Outside of getting our oldest sons together, we would meet for lunch, tennis, and celebrations. We also helped each other through some of the toughest times of our lives.

When we first became friends, I was in a controlling marriage. I desperately wanted my marriage to work out. My husband and I had two children together, and they developed medical issues, which made the idea of separation or divorce feel like it was too much to handle. My friend helped me gain the confidence and strength I needed to leave my toxic marriage.

She was diagnosed with stage IV cancer a few years after we became friends. Throughout our friendship and especially after her diagnosis, she repeatedly told me how supportive and loving her husband was with her and the kids. When she was diagnosed, he told her they were in it together. She told me (with tears in her eyes) how he "picked her up off the floor more than once." I told her how good it was for me to hear about their relationship and how she deserved it. She would look at me and tell me I deserved it, too.

She passed away on her and my oldest son's birthday. (Yes, our oldest sons have the same birthday.) Our boys, who initially brought us together with their friendship, now celebrate each birthday with loving memories of her.

At the memorial service, her widower hugged me tightly. During that moment, I felt things were different between us. His hug made me feel cared for and comforted. He had been extremely reserved with me in the past, and I was not expecting to feel such a connection with him.

A few weeks after her service, he reached out to me by inviting my son to go to a movie with him and his two boys. I gave him my address, and he laughed, telling me he knew where I lived. Later that month, he invited me and my kids to a New Year's celebration to honor his late wife with her close friends and his family. After that night, we started texting and writing to each other. We made plans together with our four kids. We went ice skating, had dinner out together, and played putt-putt. Our first "date" (time alone) was a little over two months after his wife had physically left us.

My connection with him has been the most powerful relationship I have ever had. He shared with me that when he met me, he felt I was going to be an important part of his life. He had only experienced that feeling once before—when he met his wife. He did not know what to make of the feeling when he met me, so he kept his distance from me. When my friend was sick, she told him not to wait long after she passed away to find someone new. She wanted him to find happiness without her.

When she died, she left a poem about love for him to find, and she described the love she felt from him and the love she felt from me. She did not mention my name, but he says she wrote it in a way that he would know she was thinking about me.

When we are together with our four kids, it feels spiritually-guided and easy. Most of our friends and family have been accepting of our relationship. One person told my children that my relationship with him probably began before his wife died. At first, I found that suggestion offensive, but I have come to accept that in some ways, that person is right. Our relationship began with her. In his words, "A love so powerful is transformed into something new. Things are entangled in a dimension that our eyes cannot see, but our hearts can feel."

3

FIVE RED FLAGS TO WATCH FOR WHEN DATING A WIDOWER

I'M FREQUENTLY ASKED IF A certain widower behavior, like always talking about his late wife or having photos all over the house, is a red flag that the widower isn't ready to move forward. Often, these answers aren't black and white, and much depends on the specific situation and what, if anything, the widower is doing to correct the problem. The purpose of this chapter isn't to go over every possible circumstance you might find yourself in, but to identify the five specific red flags that usually indicate the widower isn't ready for a serious relationship. If he exhibits any of these red flags, it's more than likely he's not ready to open his heart to you.

RED FLAG #1: THE WIDOWER HIDES YOU FROM FAMILY AND FRIENDS

Most widowers start dating long before their children, close friends, and family are ready to see them with other women. Because widowers think their loved ones won't support or understand their decision to date again (a decision the widowers themselves often can't explain), they often keep their dating and relationships a secret for as long as possible.

It's normal to be concerned about telling family and friends. These conversations are never easy, and it's difficult to predict how others will react to this news. But widowers who are ready to open their hearts again will find the strength and courage to do it. Not telling others about your relationship becomes a red flag when widowers continually make excuses as to why it hasn't happened yet. You'll know it's a red flag because you'll feel like a mistress or a secret girlfriend.

Never tolerate being treated like some dirty little secret. When a widower hides you and your relationship from others, what he's really saying is that he values the feelings of his loved ones more than he values you. Remember, men express their true feelings through their actions. When he intentionally hides you, keeps you from meeting loved ones, or purposely excludes you from family activities and get-togethers, what he's really saying is that you're not that important.

Over the years, I've talked with women who were literally asked to hide in a closet or wait quietly in another room when a widower's friends or family stopped by unannounced. Other times, they were introduced as "just a friend" to the widower's acquaintances. Some widowers refuse to eat at certain restaurants, shop at specific stores, or visit parts of town with their new girlfriends because they're worried about running into someone they know. Other widowers plan dates or secret rendezvous only when they don't interfere with planned family gatherings.

Widowers who are serious about opening their hearts will make introductions—no matter how difficult those announcements or meetings may be. The hardest conversation I had after dating again was telling Krista's brother and grandmother that I was in a serious relationship with Julianna. I knew they were still grieving, and it would be difficult for them to know that just seven months after their granddaughter and sister's death, I was in love again. Still, it was a conversation that needed to happen. Krista's brother and grandmother were a big part of my life for seven years, and I knew it would hurt them even more to learn about my relationship with Julianna from someone else.

The more hesitant widowers are to tell others about the women they're dating, the greater their internal doubts are about the relationship. Those who are confident about their feelings will have these conversations. For example, when Jennifer came to visit me for the first time, I waited until the last possible minute to tell my family she was coming. I *only* told them about Jennifer because I lived down the street from my parents, and there was no way I could hide the fact that I had a visitor. At the time, I rationalized my actions by telling myself I didn't want to hurt the feelings of loved ones who were still grieving.

However, when I became serious with Julianna a few months later, I *never* hid her or our relationship from anyone. In fact, I relished opportunities to introduce Julianna to everyone I knew. This change took place because I had no doubts about my feelings for Julianna. I knew I wanted to spend the rest of my life with her, and in order to do that, I had to integrate her into all aspects of my life.

By now, some of you are wondering when the widower should introduce you to friends and family. With close family members, it should happen soon after becoming exclusive. In cases where he's worried about a negative reaction, it might be better for him to inform those he loves that he's in an exclusive relationship before making face-to-face introductions. If introducing you in person isn't practical or realistic, at the very least, the widower should let them know he's in a committed relationship and who it's with.

In my situation, I thought it was better to let Krista's brother and grandmother know that I was in an exclusive relationship before they met Julianna. It was one of the most difficult conversations I've ever had. Even though they were both verbally supportive and were thankful that I had told them, I could sense that they didn't understand how I could open my heart to someone else less than a year after Krista's death. When I introduced them to Julianna a few weeks later, I could tell they were still struggling with my decision, but they were polite and welcoming. If I hadn't had that previous conversation with them, I don't believe the actual introduction would have gone nearly as well.

The only exception I make to this rule is when the widower has minor children living at home. When that's the case, I think the relationship should be on solid ground before introductions are made. This, however, doesn't give the widower license not to tell them what he's doing. At the very least, his minor children should know that their father is dating, and he should give you a rough timeline of when introductions will happen. However, if he continually makes up excuses as to why you haven't met his kids or keeps changing the deadline, he's hiding you and not ready to open his heart.

Remember that you should expect the same behavior from a widower that you would from any other man. Don't let widowers get away with treating you like a secret. You deserve and should expect to be treated like the center of his universe.

RED FLAG #2: YOU REMIND THE WIDOWER OF HIS LATE WIFE

Three months after Krista died, I created a profile on an online dating website. Back then, online dating was relatively new, and nowhere as sophisticated as the dating apps of today. After filling out some basic information about myself, I posted a single photograph, along with a paragraph about myself and what kind of woman I was looking to date. Then I started applying the website's filters to see who came back as compatible matches.

Though I didn't realize it at the time, I was inputting Krista's characteristics into the search filters, and as a result, the site was returning women who looked somewhat like Krista and had similar interests and hobbies. I didn't do this intentionally. However, at that point in my life, Krista was the only woman I'd had a serious, long-term relationship with. We clicked on so many levels that I unconsciously figured that by putting in Krista's interests and personality traits, I'd find someone who would be a good match. Despite the site returning dozens of "compatible" women, I never clicked with any of them when we met in person. At the time, I didn't understand why I couldn't connect with someone with similar looks and interests. In hindsight, I realize I wanted those women to be just like Krista and duplicate that wonderful relationship we shared.

I tell this story because when widowers start dating, their frame of reference for what makes a compatible or desirable partner is based on the looks, personality, and interests of the late wife. They think that finding someone who looks familiar and acts similarly to the late wife will heal their heart. (I recommend that widowers date several different women when they re-enter the dating waters so they'll get exposed to a diverse set of women with different personalities and interests.) I was initially attracted to Jennifer because she was very similar to Krista. Like Krista, Jennifer was tall, blonde, creative, and had an outgoing personality. We even matched up perfectly in the political and faith aspects of our lives. That alone brought me a level of comfort and familiarity that made it an easy decision to let the relationship become more serious.

The fact that you have similar looks or personality to the late wife isn't a red flag by itself. You should become concerned if the widower tries to mold you and your relationship into a replica of the one he shared with his late wife. Fortunately, this is an easy red flag to identify. The four most common things widowers who are looking to reconstruct their relationship with their late wife will do are:

1. Verbally compare the two of you. This is usually done through subtle hints about the way the late wife did things and how much he enjoyed them.

2. Constantly point out physical characteristics that you and the late wife share.

3. Ask you to dress in the late wife's clothes and/or behave like her while you're out on a date or in the bedroom.

4. Constantly take you to the same places where he and the late wife ate, vacationed, and frequented while refusing to try new things with you.

If all this sounds creepy, it is. If you find yourself dating a widower who exhibits one or more of these traits, note that healthy boundaries or better communication won't fix this. He's trying to re-create a part of his life that is gone forever by obliterating your unique personality and identity. He will never love you for who you are—only for who he thinks you can be. The best thing you can do if you find yourself in this kind of relationship is to end it immediately. In order for a relationship with a widower to grow and thrive, he has to love the new woman for who she is—not who he wants her to be. It's a lesson I didn't learn until I fell in love with Julianna.

RED FLAG #3: THE WIDOWER CONSTANTLY TALKS ABOUT THE LATE WIFE

When I started dating, I always had an urge to talk about Krista. I wanted to tell the women I dated what a fabulous person Krista was, how much I missed her, and little tidbits of information about her. For the most part, I managed to keep those thoughts to myself and focus on getting to know the woman I was dating. Still, it took a lot of energy and concentration to keep focused on my date instead of talking about Krista. To this day, I have no idea why I had that constant urge. Perhaps it was some kind of grief or coping mechanism. Whatever the reason, over the years, I've learned that other widowers have the same desire to talk about their late wives when they start dating.

This in and of itself isn't a red flag. The red flag occurs when widowers find a way to inject the late wife into every conversation or activity. Say you're driving through town together and the widower points to a restaurant and says, "My wife and I ate there all the time" or "That was my wife's favorite place to eat." You could be at home watching TV, and he comments on how his wife always liked the actor on the screen or the type of show you're watching. You could be listening to music, and the widower finds some way to tie a memory of his wife into the conversation.

While it's hard to say why widowers want to talk about their late wives, what I do know is that most of them can and will bring it under control if you let them know it bothers you. This usually involves saying something along the lines of, "I know you had a good marriage, but when you talk about your late wife all the time, it makes me feel like you're not ready to move on. I don't mind hearing about her from time to time, but let's make sure it's relevant to our conversation or what we're doing." Remember that you're not asking that he never speak of his late wife. Instead, you're asking that she only be part of a conversation when it's appropriate or relevant.

When I started dating Jennifer, I didn't talk much about Krista. As time went on, however, I talked about her more often. Jennifer never objected or expressed concern, so Krista became a more frequent part of our conversations. I don't remember talking about her all the time, but I do remember feeling that I could talk about her whenever I wanted because Jennifer didn't seem to care. It wasn't until after we broke up that I learned just how hard it was for her to hear stories about Krista.

When I was dating Julianna, I was so worried about doing or saying something that would bring our relationship to an end that I rarely, if ever, talked about Krista. It reached a point where Julianna had to let me know that it was okay to talk about Krista from time to time. There were things she wanted to know about Krista, our marriage, and Krista's suicide so she could understand me better. It took some time, but eventually I found a way to talk about Krista that worked for both of us.

Widowers who are unable to stop talking about the late wife need more help than you can give them. Even though they're with you physically, their minds are stuck in the past, unable to embrace the present and future. While it's fine to set boundaries and give these widowers a chance to improve, if he can't stop talking about his late wife, the relationship isn't worth continuing.

RED FLAG #4: HE WON'T REMOVE SHRINES TO THE LATE WIFE

It's normal for widowers to keep a shrine in memory of their late wives. Some shrines are big and obvious, like an urn displayed prominently in the home. It might be a giant photograph on the wall or a room dedicated to the late wife's things.

Other memorials to the late wife aren't so obvious. It could be a physical object like her car, her clothes, mementos from trips they took together, or even the home he and the late wife shared. If you're not sure what the shrine is, look for things he has a hard time parting with. Whatever form the shrine takes, the purpose of it is the same: to remember the late wife, honor her memory, and bring some emotional comfort to the widower.

Having a shrine in and of itself isn't a red flag. Everyone has different ways of dealing with loss, and it's natural to want to preserve the memory of the deceased. The first time you visit a widower's home and see a memorial to the late wife, don't panic and think that the widower isn't ready to date again. Perhaps you're the first date he's brought home, or maybe he hasn't found someone he loves enough to take down the memorial. Shrines only become red flags as the relationship becomes serious and he doesn't make any effort to remove them.

My memorial to Krista consisted of a dozen photographs that adorned various rooms of my house. Some photographs were large, others were small. Some photos were just of her, while others were of the two of us. You couldn't spend more than a few minutes in my house without seeing an image of Krista.

Krista's presence was something Julianna acutely felt the first time she visited my house. She didn't tell me at the time, but when she went home that night, she wondered if I was ready for the serious relationship I claimed to want, when photographs of Krista hung in practically every room of my home. The second time Julianna visited, I sensed she was uncomfortable and wondered if Krista's photos had something to do with it. Since we spent all our time in the kitchen or living room, I removed the photos of Krista in those rooms. The next time Julianna visited, I could immediately tell a difference in her demeanor. She seemed more relaxed, and stayed longer than her previous visits.

As our relationship became more serious, the rest of the photographs came down one by one. At first, taking them down wasn't easy. Putting them away was like saying goodbye to Krista. Before removing each one, I asked myself if I valued Krista's photo more than my relationship with Julie. As our love for each other grew, it became easier to take down the pictures. It took two months, but eventually, Julie could go anywhere in my house without seeing Krista looking back at her.

Widowers who are ready to open their hearts won't let shrines come between you and them. They will sell the late wife's car, scatter her ashes, take down the photos, remove the mementos, or redecorate the house. Widowers who refuse to remove shrines or talk about doing it but never take action aren't ready to move forward. They're in love with the memory of someone they'll never see again in this life. Don't trick yourself into thinking you'll get used to her pictures, her knickknacks, or the urn on the mantel, because you won't. The shrine, whatever form it takes, will gnaw at you until it drives you crazy. You can't compete with a memory. Memories always win.

RED FLAG #5: AFTER A YEAR TOGETHER, HE CAN'T SEE A FUTURE WITH YOU

I'm inevitably asked how long it takes a widower to open his heart to someone else. The answer is simple: Widowers will eagerly start a new chapter when they find a woman they want to spend the rest of their lives with. It doesn't matter how recently their wife passed away or how she died. When widowers find the right person, they'll work through their sorrow and loss and start a new life. And the best part? They know whether the woman they're dating has long-term potential usually within weeks or months of first meeting her.

Don't believe me? Ask a man who's happily married how long it took him to know that his wife was the person he wanted to spend the rest of his life with. Every one of them will tell you that they knew it within weeks or months. If you feel it's appropriate (and if you really want to know), ask your widower how quickly he knew his late wife was someone he could spend the rest of his life with. You'll get the same answer.

If you've been with a widower for a year or more and he can't commit to marriage or a long-term relationship, he'll never be able to give either of those to you. He may say that he needs more time to grieve or that he can't see a future with you now, but if you're patient just a little longer, he'll eventually work things out. No matter what a widower says to convince you to stay with him, you need to know you're in a relationship that's not going anywhere.

When a widower meets a woman he wants to spend the rest of his life with, he will do—not say—whatever it takes to make that woman the love of his life. He will take down the photos of the late wife, scatter her ashes, stop posting on social media about her, sell their home, introduce the new woman to family and friends, and figure out the best way to blend families. He won't make excuses or say that he needs more time to grieve. While there's bound to be bumps and setbacks along the way, the relationship won't stay in a rut for months or years on end. Widowers will try hard to make things work if they want a lifelong relationship with you.

About a month after Krista and I started dating, I knew I could happily spend the rest of my life with her. I had never felt that way about anyone else before, and part of me wondered if this feeling was real or if it would fade as our relationship matured. It never did. In fact, the more time I spent with Krista, the more I could see us getting married, having children, and growing old together. And though I figured there would hardships and the normal ups and downs that everyone experiences, I wanted to do it with Krista by my side.

I never felt that way with Jennifer. I enjoyed her company and had a good time when we were together, but something about the relationship didn't feel right. At the time, I thought it was because I was recently widowed and grieving. Once I worked through that, I'd be able to see us starting a family and growing old together.

It never happened.

Whenever Jennifer brought up the subject of marriage and our future together, I'd nod along with her and talk about the future she envisioned even though I could never see myself as her husband.

Then Julianna came along, and everything changed.

Even though our first date was a disaster, I sensed there was something special about her. Those feelings were strong enough for me to ask for a second chance. After our next date, I knew Julianna was someone I could marry, start a family with, and spend the rest of my life with. In fact, the love I had for Julianna was the same love I felt toward Krista.

Yes, you read that right. My feelings for Krista and Julianna were one and the same.

Despite those similarities, I wasn't sure if I could trust my feelings. I was still an emotional mess and wondered if my feelings for Julianna were temporary and would fade once the honeymoon phase of our relationship wore off. Besides, we started dating just as my relationship with Jennifer was ending. I hadn't crossed any grief milestones or made any major progress on opening my heart. There was no logical reason why I could suddenly open my heart to someone else. However, the more time I spent with Julianna, the stronger my feelings about her became. Within a month, I knew I wanted to marry her. (It took Julianna a bit longer to feel the same way.)

Julianna didn't say or do anything special that made me fall in love with her. There was just something wonderful about her that reinforced itself whenever I spent time with her. Because of this, I was determined to show her that I was ready to start a new chapter of my life, so I started making changes. Nine months after our disastrous first date, we exchanged vows and became husband and wife.

Some of you are probably thinking that my story is unique. After all, I was young when I was widowed and didn't have to deal with the issues and stress that come with blending families. In reality, it doesn't matter how old the widower is, how many kids he has, or how long he and the late wife were married. Over the last fifteen years, I've witnessed this pattern of widowers knowing they've found someone special repeated over and over and over again, and their love for this new woman doesn't fade. Instead, it grows stronger and stronger as the relationship becomes more serious.

For those who are wondering if there's something you can do or say to help the widower see what a catch you are, the only thing you can do is be yourself. That alone should be all the motivation the widower needs to move forward. If he doesn't see it, it's his loss, not yours.

EMMA'S STORY

I had a three-year relationship with my widower that ended twenty-five years ago. We both went on to have great lives, crossing paths amicably only twice. He was married fourteen years, and I remained single.

I had no idea his wife had been ill until accidentally finding her online obituary from thirteen months prior. I sent him a condolence card, and it prompted him to send a note asking me out for coffee. That meet-up twenty-seven months ago lasted seven hours. We laughed, cried, and shared photos of grown kids and new grandkids. I welcomed stories about his late wife from the man whose heart was still in pieces, and as I listened, my heart hurt for him.

The beginnings of our relationship were too quick for me. He was ready to move forward with a "known commodity." Me? Overly cautious with respect for the grieving process stages. Quite frankly, I wasn't sure I even wanted a boyfriend.

His house was a shrine, with dozens of photographs in every room, love notes, trinkets from vacations, etc. Her obituary described their "love of the ages" and outlined her many professional and athletic talents. She would be a hard act to follow, whomever his future partner might be.

After enlisting a counselor to learn how best to navigate this unknown emotional territory, my therapist hit me between the eyes when he told me I was seeing a married man. Boy, was he right. In hindsight, I should have told him to get in touch in a year. But I didn't. He was still very much in love, and it broke my heart to watch.

I treaded slowly and cautiously while he planned vacations more than a year out and was under the impression that we were a solid couple. Could we be, given that his heart was elsewhere? I loved him, but in a very guarded way. I was always comparing my klutzy self to the accomplished athlete I'd been told was a bright light in the room. I felt second best.

Our first year together, I listened to endless stories about her illness, his off-the-charts loving care, honoring her wishes, their mini vacations timed between treatments, how close they thought they were to the cure, etc. I hiked where they sprinkled her ashes, left him heartfelt notes on key anniversaries, and met her best friends, who shared stories about how wonderful she was. My counselor told me I knew too much about her and the life they shared together. While the widower sweetly and proudly called me a "girlfriend," I wondered if I was more of a grief counselor of sorts as he moved forward (not on) in his life. All this was emotionally exhausting and taking its toll. Somewhere, I forgot to set boundaries.

Her photos, seventy-five in all—yes, I counted— represented a work-hard-play-hard life well-lived. I tolerated them, since I wasn't all in yet anyway and considered it not my place to expect more. I simply asked him for empathy for what I felt when entering the home she designed and decorated.

As we entered the second year together, I was more vocal about the photos. If we were to move forward, they had to be addressed. There were fifteen to twenty photos in the master suite alone. One of them had her in a big smile, staring at me in bed. Another ten of their wedding and on-his-knee proposal within plain view. Yes, I, this strong and independent, financially secure, fully capable sixty-something woman put up with that for way too long. Hindsight being 20/20, I respected the widower and the late wife more than I did myself.

In response to my request, he moved two or three from direct view, but left the rest. As a result, the photos became symbols of disrespect for my wishes and feelings. Finally, he moved them to rooms I don't frequent. My friends, family, and support group tribe can't believe I'm still here. At times, neither can I. The counselor opined that a human's need for connection trumps a lot—after all, we have common hobbies, travel well together, and he's a good man! Could the "net net" be a good friend and travel partner, even if we aren't a couple? I wish I knew.

RACHEL'S STORY

When John and I began dating, he told me how much he loved and adored his folks—and how much they would love me. While they lived hundreds of miles away, they were a tight-knit family, even more so following Kristen's death two years earlier. I was excited to meet them.

When I arrived at John's house—the same house he shared with Kristen—his parents greeted me with smiles and open arms. His stepmom, Carol, asked about my favorite movie, my favorite books, my hobbies.

"Those were Kristen's favorites, too," she said.

I felt my face flush at the mention of Kristen's name, but I also felt a strange kinship to the woman who came before me.

Maybe our similarities bode well for my relationship with Carol, I thought.

I soon realized that Carol was still reliving every memory, every moment, every facet of Kristen's life, even celebrating John and Kristen's anniversary with dinner at their reception site, followed by a viewing of their wedding video late into the night. Even worse, Carol always addressed Kristen as "you know who" when I was in the room. I felt like she was pitting me against Kristen, expecting that the mere mention of her name would make me feel weak and insecure. And it did, but only because Carol ensured that every conversation evolved into a tribute to Kristen. When I changed the subject, Carol lost interest. But instead of bowing out of the conversation, I found myself comforting Carol, indulging her stories and asking questions about Kristen. I learned that was the *only* way I could connect with Carol. At the time, it didn't occur to me that her behavior was inappropriate, or that playing the role of psychologist for my future mother-in-law wasn't healthy for either one of us.

This twisted relationship turned toxic almost immediately after John and I got engaged. When I called Carol to share my joy and excitement, 95% of our conversation was about Kristen and her marriage to John. Instead of setting boundaries and shifting the conversation onto more neutral ground, I fed into Carol's grief, promising to honor Kristen's memory.

"It's great that you're not intimidated by a ghost," she said, while at the same time placing Kristen on an unattainable pedestal.

Things continued to get worse. Thankfully, John stood up for me. He told his parents that unless they could respect the two of us and the lives we were building together, they weren't welcome in our home or in our lives.

I never became a saint like Kristen, but I did gain wings. I learned to stand up for myself, establish boundaries, and no longer cater to Carol's needs at the expense of my own. My in-laws' home will continue to be adorned with pictures of Kristen and John on their wedding day, with nary a photo of John and me in sight. They'll continue to talk to John only on holidays. When *he* calls. And even though John and I have been married for two years, they will do their best to pretend I don't exist. And you know what? I'm okay with that.

While I don't have the fantasy in-laws I pictured when John raved about his folks during our courtship, my marriage is better than I ever imagined—in part because we learned to cope with adversity before we even said "I do." Carol has chosen to live in the past, where her relationship with Kristen is completely intact. John and I are stepping into the future, celebrating every day we have together and hoping maybe one day, she'll join us.

4

THE TWO BIG MISTAKES WOMEN MAKE WHEN DATING A WIDOWER

THE FIRST THREE CHAPTERS IN this book discussed widower behavior and psychology so you can better discern whether they're ready to open their hearts. In this chapter, we'll switch focus and discuss the two big mistakes women make when dating widowers.

Before we dive into these mistakes, don't be discouraged if you've made one or both of them. If you've never dated a widower before, it's difficult to know what is appropriate and acceptable to ask of him. Instead of feeling bad about past mistakes you've made, take what you learn in this chapter as an opportunity to improve your relationship and communication skills. I've seen many widower relationships that were hanging by a thread turn into marriages or lifelong partnerships once these mistakes were corrected. But even if your relationship with the widower doesn't work out, correcting these mistakes will improve your mental and emotional health and benefit you in future romantic relationships.

MISTAKE #1: THE WIDOWERHOOD EXCUSE

Let's say you meet a recent widower through a dating app. After getting to know each other online, you agree to meet in person. When you meet him, you're surprised to see that he's still wearing his wedding band.

What would you do next?

Would you tell him that you don't date married men and ask him to remove it? Would you shrug it off and figure it's not a big deal? Would you keep quiet and hope he removes it before you meet him a second time?

If you're not sure exactly what you'd do or say in this situation, that's normal. Every woman who dates a widower eventually runs into a widower-related issue where they're not sure how to respond. Many of you probably have at least one specific example that popped into your mind as you began this chapter.

While not knowing how to respond to situations you've never encountered before is normal, the first mistake women make is not speaking up or setting boundaries when the situation presents itself a second time. Keeping quiet when you would normally speak up or excusing behaviors from widowers that you wouldn't tolerate from other men you date is what I call the Widowerhood Excuse. It happens because women aren't sure what widower behavior is "normal" or if it's even appropriate to ask a man who has lost his wife to change his conduct.

Let's go back to the wedding band example I used earlier, but make one small change to the situation. What if the man wearing the wedding band was single or divorced? Would you ask him why he was wearing it or tell him there wasn't going to be a date unless he removed it? For most women, the answer would be yes. But when it's a widower, most people aren't sure what to do. Some women see the ring as a sign that he really loved his late wife. Others don't like it, but are unsure of how to bring it up or worry about offending the widower if they ask about it. And some keep quiet and hope he'll eventually remove the ring on his own once a serious relationship begins.

Whatever your reason for not speaking up, allowing behavior that you normally wouldn't tolerate because of the widower's loss is bad for the relationship and even worse for your emotional and mental health. In addition, widowers will interpret your silence as acceptance. If you don't speak up and say anything about the ring or anything else that's bothering you, the widower will think you don't have a problem with it. And the longer you remain silent, the more difficult it becomes for widowers to change.

When I was dating Jennifer, I eventually realized that she was letting me get away with behavior she normally wouldn't tolerate. For example, I had a tendency to talk about Krista even when there wasn't a reason to bring her up. Jennifer never said or did anything that indicated she didn't want to hear stories about my late wife. Other times, my emotions would get the better of me, and I'd break down in tears. Again, Jennifer never said anything about how much this bothered her. Without any pushback from

Jennifer, I simply assumed that my behavior didn't bother her. (It wouldn't be until months after we broke up that I learned just how hard it was for her to hear stories about Krista or to try to be supportive when I was an emotional mess.)

It wasn't that way with Julianna. She made it very clear that she expected the same behavior from me as she would any other guy she dated. Since I was dating again, she expected me to focus on building a relationship instead of using our time together as a therapy session. While she didn't expect me to forget about the past or Krista, she wasn't going to lower her standards and tolerate feeling like second place just because I had lost a spouse. When issues or concerns did come up, she addressed them in a loving, but firm, way.

I've coached women who put up with bad and unhealthy behavior from widowers for years because they didn't think they could say anything, or they thought the widowers' behaviors would change once they stopped grieving. Don't be quiet. Speak up. Losing a spouse is an awful, gut-wrenching experience, but that doesn't give widowers license to behave badly or treat you poorly. If you're not sure what healthy boundaries are or how to set them with widowers, this next section will answer all your questions.

MISTAKE #2: NOT SETTING HEALTHY BOUNDARIES

All healthy relationships have boundaries. Boundaries "protect our sense of personal identity and help guard against being overwhelmed by the demands of others."[4]

Yet when dating widowers, many women hesitate to set any boundaries. Reasons for this vary. Sometimes, they think the widower should simply know how to behave, and they shouldn't have to say anything. Others think that it's insensitive or heartless to ask a widower to change when he's lost a spouse. Some are concerned that speaking up and setting boundaries will end the relationship. Whatever the reason for keeping quiet, not setting healthy boundaries is the second big mistake women make when dating a widower. You must set boundaries if the relationship is going to have any chance of working out.

Setting boundaries with a widower is often intimidating because you're asking him to change something that relates to his marriage or his late wife. For example, asking widowers to remove wedding bands is asking them to take off their outward symbol of love and devotion. That can seem like a big thing to ask, and it sometimes is. However, if you don't set boundaries, the behavior won't change, and whatever is bothering you will eventually drive you crazy.

In order to set healthy boundaries, the first thing you need to do is figure out what you can actually live with. While some issues, like wearing a wedding band, are more black and white, other issues, like whether to allow any photos of the late wife on the wall, might require more thought. If you're not sure, take time to think about what you can and can't live with. And while there's not one right answer to some of these widower-related issues, what's important is that you don't lie to yourself about what's acceptable. For example, if you can't live with *any* photographs of the late wife on the wall, you need to be honest with yourself and the widower about your feelings.

The second reason for setting healthy boundaries is that if you don't speak up, widowers will likely think you're fine with the way things are. Many of you who just read that last sentence are probably thinking, how can a man *not* know that the ring on his hand or photos bother the woman he's dating? There are two reasons for this. First, if you watch men who are good friends interact, you'll notice that they tend to be upfront and straightforward with each other. They don't have a problem telling one of their buddies when they don't like something he did or said. That's the way men are inclined to speak to each other, and it's generally the language they understand best. If you don't speak up, widowers take your silence as a kind of unspoken agreement that you're okay with things.

The second reason is that widowers often don't see the world the way you see it. For example, when you walk through his house, all you can see are the smiling photos of the late wife staring back at you. Widowers, on the other hand, probably aren't giving these photos a second thought. To them, the photographs have hung on the walls for years and are simply part of the background. You need to speak up and share your thoughts so they can see the world through your eyes. Most widowers will take off their wedding rings and make their homes a more comfortable place for the women they're dating once they know how you feel. But the key is to speak up and set those boundaries. Otherwise, the chances of anything changing are zero.

Setting boundaries gives widowers a chance to decide if they're really ready to open their hearts. In Chapter 2, you read that men need a reason to change their behavior. If you're not setting boundaries with a widower, you're not giving him a chance to decide if he values you over the photographs on the wall, the wedding band on his finger, or whatever else is bothering you.

So, how do you set healthy boundaries? Let me show you how Julianna did it. When we started dating, there were lots of red flags that I wasn't ready for a serious relationship: I wore my wedding band on a chain around my neck, there were photos of Krista on every wall of my home, and when I talked about Krista, I referred to her as "my wife." Julianna had never considered dating a widower, and until we started spending time together, she had never given any of these issues a second thought. At first, Julianna was unsure what, if anything, she could ask me to change or if these were issues she wanted to deal with. Several times, she came close to ending the relationship because she thought it would be easier to date someone who didn't come with all the widower baggage.

To make matters worse, Julianna didn't have any friends or family members who had experience dating a widower. There was no one who could tell her whether my behavior was normal or what boundaries she should set. The internet was still in its infancy, and her numerous Google searches came back with no books, support groups, or other resources that could guide her along the path of dating a widower. Thankfully, before she gave up, she decided to see if setting firm but healthy boundaries would yield any results.

The first issue she tackled was always referring to Krista as "my wife." Julianna didn't know how she wanted me to refer to Krista, but she knew that "my wife" wasn't acceptable, as that made her feel she was dating a married man. The next time I used the words "my wife" when referring to Krista, she started setting healthy boundaries. Our conversation went something like this:

Julianna: Just so you know, it makes me really uncomfortable when you call Krista your wife. I know you love her and that you had this great life together, but it makes me feel like I'm dating a married man when you refer to her that way. I don't date married men. Is there some other way you can refer to her?

Me: (pausing for a moment) Oh, I didn't know that bothered you.

Julianna: It does. A lot.

Me: What do you want me to call her?

Julianna: (pausing for a moment) I don't know. Just not your wife.

Me: (thinking) I don't have any ideas.

Julianna: I wish I had some, but I don't. All I know is that if this relationship is going to work out, we need to come up with something else.

Me: I don't have a solution off the top of my head. Let me think about it for a day or two.

Julianna: That would be great. Thanks for understanding.

Though I didn't tell Julianna at the time, I was offended that she wanted me to refer to Krista as something other than my wife, especially when she didn't have an alternative suggestion. However, until Julianna raised the issue, I had no idea that referring to Krista as "my wife" bothered her. (Yes, I really was that clueless.) Neither Jennifer nor any of the other women I dated had ever said anything about it, so I thought it was fine to refer to Krista in that manner. Julianna's request, however, started me thinking about other ways I could refer to Krista, and whether my relationship with Julianna was worth making that change.

After our conversation, I went home. I thought over her concerns and decided that I loved Julianna enough to change the way I referred to Krista. By the time we got together the next day, I had some solutions to run past her. Our conversation went something like this:

> **Me:** I thought about the way I refer to Krista, and I came up with two ideas. What if I refer to her either by her first name or use the term "late wife" instead?
>
> **Julianna:** (thinks about it for a long moment) You know what, that's a good idea. I think I can be okay with that. Let's try it out and see how it goes.
>
> **Me:** (relieved) I don't know how fast my brain will make the change. I still might refer to Krista as my wife from time to time.
>
> **Julianna:** That's okay. I don't expect you to be perfect at it. I just want to see that you're doing your best to move forward.

After working on that issue and seeing success, Julianna began setting boundaries, one at a time, for other widower-related issues, such as the ring around my neck. Together, we came up with solutions that were acceptable to both of us. This helped us learn how to communicate with each other about our concerns, and it drew us closer together as a couple. It taught us that if we wanted this relationship to work, we both had to be able to talk to and work with each other on this journey that neither of us had taken before.

Healthy boundaries usually work best when the widower takes responsibility for coming up with a solution instead of being told how to solve the problem. Most men bristle when they're told how to fix something and would rather figure out a solution on their own. For example, instead of telling a widower to take off his wedding band, tell him that when he wears his ring, it makes you feel like you're dating a married man. This approach lets him know how you feel and allows him to solve the problem. In addition, when *he* comes up with the solution, he can't come back later and say he was only doing what you asked him to do. There are a few exceptions to this rule, but as a general practice, letting the widower think through the problem and come up with his own answer usually works the best.

If he says he doesn't know what to do, be prepared to give him several suggestions. For example, if the late wife's clothes are still in the closet and the widower says he doesn't know the best way to dispose of them, suggest giving them to a thrift store or having his adult children sort through them. Please note that you aren't telling him how to solve the problem or what to do with the clothes, but simply planting ideas in his mind so he can figure out an answer. It's important that he come up with the solution, or at some point—usually during a fight or stressful time in the relationship—he'll blame you for making him do something he never wanted to do in the first place.

In addition, healthy boundaries only work if the widower knows there are consequences if he does nothing. For example, let's say the widower has the late wife's photograph on the nightstand, her clothes in the closet, and her toiletries still in the bathroom. When you explain your feelings to the widower, it's important to let him know that until he solves the problem, there won't be any more sex or sleepovers until you feel comfortable in his room. However, if you're back in bed with him the next night and nothing's changed, the widower will think you weren't serious about how much her photograph and clothes bother you. Julianna always let me know in a kind and loving way that she had no qualms about ending the relationship if she didn't feel like I was ready to open my heart. It was a consequence I never wanted to test.

Finally, remember that boundaries need to be realistic. For example, when Julianna asked me not to call Krista "my wife," that was a healthy boundary to set. If she had asked me never to talk about Krista at all, that would have been an unhealthy boundary, and an impossible one to keep. In coaching sessions, I've talked with women who want widowers to delete all their past social media photos of themselves with their late wives. While that might be a healthy boundary if the widower spends lots of time looking at past photos on Facebook or is constantly sharing memories of himself and the late wife, it's not a healthy request if the widower doesn't look at the photos or share memories of the past.

Remember that the purpose of boundaries isn't to eliminate all signs of his past or his relationship with his late wife, but to build a foundation on which the two of you can have a serious, loving, long-term relationship. The sooner you set healthy boundaries in the relationship, the easier it is for the widower to decide if he's ready to open his heart. The longer the widower wears his wedding band or leaves the photos up because you remain quiet, the more difficult it will be for him to adjust. The transition won't always be smooth, and most widowers will try to test your boundaries to see how serious you are about them, but those who are ready to love again will show great strides in correcting the problems.

Remember that you deserve to be treated with the same respect that the widower showed his late wife. If she didn't have to feel like a third wheel in the relationship, there's no reason for you to feel that way. Don't settle for anything less than first.

LEAH'S STORY

My Cowboy and I were married not quite six months after his late wife passed. I can say that setting healthy and realistic boundaries and expectations is crucial to your relationship and your health. I failed miserably in this, as I didn't fully understand the importance of having my expectations and boundaries respected. I gave him the non-verbal permission to dismiss my needs and desires and rights as his wife, and he took full advantage of it. I don't believe he did it to be malicious, but simply because I allowed it to occur.

This has caused such a great deal of pain and heartache that, sadly, I'm still not certain of the outcome. I allowed Cowboy to give me his late wife's wedding stone, and while it was placed in a new setting for me, it is still hers, and that continues to remain an issue. When Cowboy told me that wearing her expensive clothes was not meant to re-create her, just that they were expensive and he didn't want them to go to waste, I should have told him that I am not her and will not wear her clothes. When Cowboy told me that I don't have the right to touch anything in the home without asking him first, I should have said, "Then this can never be my home," and walked out the door. Now, a year later, my six-year-old son cannot get into his closet because there are saddles, tack, and 60-plus-year-old toys that he can't play with or touch. His clothes hang at an odd angle in the closet because it is filled with her stuff and old clothes.

I am hard-pressed to be as patient and compassionate as I once was. And when I consider her house and her things and having her ashes sit on the floor in the living room, I am reminded that I allowed this to happen to me because I didn't clearly state that these things are not acceptable. I am not saying that he didn't have the right to grieve or even keep some of her belongings, as I realize that we married very shortly after her death. But when Cowboy didn't do what I thought he would in moving past these things in a reasonable timeframe, it became painfully obvious to me that he had no intention of putting her and her things in a respectable place and allowing me to move into his heart and his home as his only wife. Now, we are at an impasse, and without his willingness to acknowledge that we need help, I'm not certain of what will become of us.

I have repeatedly requested that we seek out help, but he adamantly refuses, believing that he doesn't need any sort of help. In fact, he tells me that if I reach out for help, our marriage is over. I am heartbroken over this and continue to pray that the Holy Spirit intervenes. I'm hopeful, but I am aware now that being hopeful doesn't mean that I sit by and allow Cowboy to treat me in such a disrespectful manner. I cannot say what will occur, but I know that my being idle now only continues to allow him to behave in a very unloving, un-Christlike, un-husbandlike way, and I know that I must now take the steps to establish boundaries that I never established before and allow the proverbial chips to fall where they may.

I can say with great confidence that having many serious conversations prior to becoming deeply involved and prior to marrying a widower is absolutely necessary. One should absolutely determine where he is emotionally and if he fully understands that to move on with a new covenant means to release the old one.

ANGELA'S STORY

How I knew it was the end: We were together three years, and deep down in my heart, I knew he didn't love me the way a man should love a woman. He didn't look at me the way a man who loves a woman with his whole soul looks at a woman. He had a steel wall 10 feet high around him, and I had no hope of ever breaking that down. He would spend hours in a different room from me, and when I would hear that door close, my eyes would well with tears of sadness, rejection, and loneliness.

For three years, I walked into a home that was supposed to be "ours" and saw nothing but a home filled with W and LW's stuff. "Our" living room was filled with things they bought on their honeymoon. "Our" kitchen was filled with their dishes and pottery proclaiming her love for him. "Our" refrigerator was plastered with pictures of them, looking so in love—a look we never had. "Our" hallway had eight pictures of her hanging, and none of us. "Our" house was filled with their life, while my life sat in boxes in the basement. I would bring my stuff up, only to hear there was no room and I was too sensitive and needed to get over my issues. I asked him once to take down some of her pictures and make "our" house more about us and less about them. He screamed at me, ripped her pictures up, and didn't talk to me for two days. This was two years into the relationship.

I pleaded with him to spend holidays with me instead of her family. He would say he could never imagine hurting them and then leave for their house, breaking my heart into pieces as the door slammed shut. Her family put me down and degraded me, and he blamed it on me. "Well, I guess because of your attitude, I will be going to family functions alone from now on," is what I heard after complaining because her mom spent the whole night talking about how amazing her daughter was.

I cried night after night alone in the bed we were supposed to share. The couch received all his love at night and kept him warm when it should have been my body. How did I know it was the end? I knew the moment I started dating him. I believed he was damaged and I could fix him, heal him, and that I could be so good to him that he would fall in love with me. Instead, he left me with nothing but broken promises, a broken heart, and the shame of knowing I had just wasted three years of my life with someone incapable of loving anyone but her.

5

THE CONFIDENCE GAME

WIDOWERS, LIKE ALL MEN, ARE initially attracted to the surface-level details of the women they meet. These can include a woman's hair color or body shape, the clothes she's wearing, her sense of humor, the smell of her perfume, or even the sound of her voice. This is just how men are wired. For widowers looking for a fling or temporary companionship, surface-level details are all they care about. But for widowers who are looking for a serious relationship, they take a deeper look before deciding if the woman they're dating is worth the long-term investment of their time and energy.

The very first thing widowers look for in women is confidence.

Let me repeat that.

Widowers who are ready to open their hearts and start a new chapter in their lives are attracted to women who feel good about themselves. Period. If you come across as needy or insecure, you're more likely to attract widowers who are only looking for companionship or for a temporary fill-in rather than those who want a serious, long-term relationship.

Confident women know their value and self-worth and act in ways that convey this to others. These women know they deserve the same respect and appreciation from widowers as they do from single or divorced men, and they don't excuse behavior just because a man is a widower. Confident women don't settle for second place in a widowers' hearts, because they know that they deserve to be number one with whomever they're dating. Confident women expect to be treated like queens, and if widowers treat them like trash, they're not afraid to end the relationship and move on.

The problem, as many of you are thinking, is that dating widowers comes with unique issues that don't come with dating single or divorced men. Because of these issues, it's difficult to feel confident and good about yourself. Despite these unique situations, it's vital that you find a way to act confident—even if that means faking it temporarily—because widowers will not open their hearts and get into a long-term relationship with women who are insecure.

The challenge I've seen isn't that women lacked confidence when the relationship started, but that their confidence waned as they ran into one widower-related issue after another. For example, in my coaching sessions, I usually start by asking the women to tell me about themselves. I listen as they talk about their successful careers, the joy they find in motherhood and their family, and their activities and service to their communities. As they talk about themselves, I hear pride, joy, and self-respect in their voices. However, when the conversation shifts to widower relationship issues, the confidence in their voices vanishes.

The good news is that if you don't feel confident in your current relationship, it's possible to regain it. To do that, you'll have to do three things.

1. KNOW YOUR UNIQUE VALUE AND WORTH

Our self-worth is how we value ourselves as a person. It's not based on what others think or say about us or external factors like our career, the home we live in, or our net worth. It is internal, inherent, and unconditional. As one psychologist put it, "Self-worth is about who you are, not about what you do."[5] Your confidence is directly tied to your self-worth.

We are constantly under pressure to reevaluate our self-worth. This comes in the form of peer pressure from friends, coworkers, and loved ones, or status symbols like occupation, educational degrees, the house, neighborhood, and city we live in, the car we drive, and the clothes we wear. When we let external forces define our self-worth, our self-confidence is bound to crumble because the values and opinions of others constantly change. What's popular and hip today is mocked and laughed at tomorrow. Real self-worth is based on values and truths we know about ourselves. These values and truths rarely, if ever, change.

When our self-worth takes a beating, we lose sight of who we are and what we value. It helps to take a step back and reaffirm our inner values. I've known coworkers and friends who based most of their self-worth on their title at work and their career. When they're laid off, fired, or don't receive a promotion, their self-worth is destroyed. Eventually, most of them were able to pick themselves up and pursue bigger and better things, but it only happened *after* they centered their self-worth around their unique value instead of their job. Similarly, I've coached women who lost most of their self-worth as widower issues continued to go unresolved, only to regain it once they end the relationship for good and put some time and distance between themselves and the widower.

A good way to rediscover who you are and what you value is to find a quiet place where you can be alone and think. Turn off your phone and give yourself time to ponder the following questions:

1. What are my long-term goals in a relationship? Are the widower's long-term goals aligned with mine? If they're not, will I be happy settling for less than what I want?

2. How do I expect the men I date (widowed or otherwise) to treat me? Does the widower treat me the way I expect to be treated? Does the way the widower treats me increase or decrease my self-worth?

3. Does the widower exhibit behaviors that I'm overlooking? Do I make excuses for these red flags because of his loss?

Based on the answers, start setting healthy boundaries with the widower. If he respects you, he'll honor those boundaries. If he doesn't respect your limits, your best course of action is to end the relationship. Either way, your self-worth will dramatically improve.

2. STOP COMPARING YOURSELF TO THE LATE WIFE

When someone dies, they become a saint. It doesn't matter if they were a drug addict, severely mentally ill, or mistreated everyone they loved. Once someone dies, those who knew and loved that person tend to forget the bad or abusive behavior and focus only on the good times and memories. This, of course, makes it difficult to hear about the late wife, because whenever she comes up in conversation, all you hear about is how kind, wonderful, and generous she was. You rarely, if ever, hear about the mistakes she made.

My late wife, Krista, killed herself when she was seven months pregnant. The last month or two of our marriage was a complete hell for me as her personality changed and she spiraled deeper and deeper into darkness. Yet whenever someone said something about Krista, there was never any mention of her crazy, unstable behavior. Instead, everyone talked about her outgoing personality, what a great writer she was, and how much fun she was to be around. All the positive things about Krista were extremely difficult for Julianna to hear because she often felt like she would never be able to measure up to Krista. Feeling compared—even when there was no intention of comparing the two of them—was difficult for Julianna to deal with, and it sometimes made her wonder if she should find another man to date who didn't have all my baggage. It took some time, but eventually Julianna realized I didn't expect her to be like Krista and that I love her for who she is. Once she was able to stop comparing herself to Krista, she felt better about herself, and it was easier for her to deal with widower-related issues when they came up.

It's normal to feel compared to the "perfect, saintly" late wife. If you're engaging in that behavior, don't be too hard on yourself. A lot of the time, the comparisons are all in our heads. Someone may tell a story that makes you compare yourself to the late wife, when the storyteller had no intention of doing so. Unless your widower is openly comparing the two of you or trying to mold you into his late wife (see Chapter 2), know that the late wife was just as human as you are and after you die, people will have nothing but good things to say about you, too.

Instead of comparing yourself, be proud of the talents and abilities that make you unique and special. Widowers who are ready to open their hearts again will love you for who you are—not who you are not.

3. OVERCOME YOUR FEAR OF LOSS

Even if women are able to regain much of their lost confidence, many still hesitate to set healthy boundaries because they're afraid such actions will result in the end of the relationship. This fear of loss stops them from taking the necessary steps to bring the relationship back into a healthy balance. They rationalize that if they give widowers more time to grieve, the widowers will eventually embrace the new relationship.

In reality, that never happens.

In Chapter 2, we learned that widowers will only change their lives if they have a reason to make a change. Setting healthy boundaries gives the widower a chance to decide what's more important: respecting your wants and needs, or the status quo. As heartbreaking as it is for any relationship to end, if the widower can't respect your boundaries, the relationship was bound to end eventually, anyway.

It takes two people to make a relationship last and endure to the end. In this book, I've told lots of stories about my long-distance relationship with Jennifer and how I dumped her after Julianna came into my life. Many of you probably wonder if the relationship with Jennifer would have worked out if I'd never met Julianna. The answer is no. The relationship with Jennifer would have eventually ended. It probably would have limped along another six months or so, but eventually, one of us would have called it off.

It's emotionally wrenching when relationships end, and no one enjoys picking up the pieces and putting their life back together. However, breaking off a relationship with someone who's not fully invested in your life, your happiness, and your future isn't a loss, but a victory.

Let me repeat that.

Breaking up with a widower who's not willing to make you the principal person in his life isn't a defeat, but a triumph. Don't prolong relationships that were never meant to last. The sooner they end, the better it is for everyone.

4. FAKE IT UNTIL YOU MAKE IT

One of the qualities that first attracted me to Julianna was the confidence she radiated. It was something I picked up on before we had spoken a single word to each other. There was something about the way she carried herself that made me think she had her act together. My feelings were confirmed as I asked people at church and some friends about her. From them, I learned that she had recently graduated from college with a degree in chemistry, and she had her own apartment and a good job—things she had accomplished at the age of twenty-three. I found all this incredibly sexy. (To put this in perspective, most of the women I dated before Julianna were in their mid-to-late twenties, and none of them had reached that level of achievement and independence.)

Because of the confidence she radiated, I realized that having a shot at a serious relationship with her would require me to up my game. Though I wasn't sure what upping my game entailed, I knew Julianna wasn't just going to give me her heart. It would require a lot of work to earn her attention and affection.

As we dated, Julianna's confidence never wavered, or so it appeared. It wasn't until sometime after we were married that I learned Julianna lost a lot of her confidence as she learned about Krista and encountered widower-related issues. Several times, it reached a point where she came close to ending our relationship because she was tired of feeling compared or thinking she'd never have the number one place in my heart. But despite her lack of confidence, she did a great job of faking it. Even though we had numerous conversations where Julianna expressed her worries and concerns, my progress (or lack thereof), and her expectations, I never sensed that she was desperate or unsure of herself. If anything, her faux confidence reinforced the notion that if I didn't get my act together, Julianna would walk and not look back.

Thankfully, as I made progress on these issues, her confidence grew. By the time we got engaged six months after our first date, her confidence had returned, and she no longer had to fake it. She felt good about herself and spending the rest of her life with me.

If you're not feeling confident for whatever reason, fake it. Widowers won't be able to tell whether your confidence is real or not. Confidence, even the fake kind, will weed out those widowers who are only looking for companionship. These widowers know that unconfident women are more likely to tolerate photos on the wall, them talking about their late wife, or feeling like second place than those who appear to have a good sense of self-worth.

So be confident in who you are—even if you have to fake it for a while. Be confident in yourself and the things you say. Act like you don't need him even if you're worried that things will end, because I guarantee your confidence (or lack thereof) will have a huge impact on determining if the relationship will become serious or something he'll toss away when another woman attracts his attention.

MADELYN'S STORY

It was his wife's robe, hanging on a hook in the bathroom, that ended our romance. I hadn't meant to date someone who was involved with another. Call me old-fashioned, but I'm not into threesomes, and I have enough self-respect not to cast myself as the "other woman."

My first date with Will was great. We went to dinner and didn't stop talking for a good three hours. During that date, Will told me about his late wife, Christine, how they had been married for 40 years, and that she had died of cancer two-and-a-half years ago. However, when Will talked about his home, he referred to it as "their" house and where "they" lived. A little confused, I tried to clarify if there was someone he lived with, but he insisted there wasn't anyone else. When I finally went to his house, the living room was one that had been preserved, almost eerily so, since the day Christine had died. There were easily 20 pictures of the woman spanning their entire married life displayed on every piece of furniture, wall, nook, and cranny.

Our relationship progressed, and over the next few months, Will and I saw each other several times per week. I enjoyed his company and craved our incredible sexual encounters, but felt that there was a part of him that was absent—present but not accounted for. I also questioned his allegiance. His constant use of plural pronouns and references to Christine made me think that he'd give anything to have her back in his life. Given that he couldn't make that happen, I wondered if I was a mere consolation prize. Wasn't I worth more?

It was a Sunday morning after we had made love. Will always wore a gold necklace with a medal on it, and I had never really looked at it closely before. I asked him about it now, and he told me that it was a medal of St. Christopher, then explained that his wife had wanted a St. Christopher's medal after completing her first bout of chemotherapy. They had searched and searched for just the right medal until they found this one. St. Christopher is the patron saint of travelers, and Christine wanted to be protected by her namesake for whatever lay ahead.

It was a very touching story, but the weird vibes descended upon me again, this time in a heavy shroud. Was Christine somehow with us every time we had sex? Was she somehow hypnotizing me when Will and I were doing it?

I went to the bathroom. I looked up at the two bathrobes hooked to the back of the door, and I couldn't help but ask Will if one of the robes was Christine's. He said it was. She had been dead two-and-a-half years and still had a hook in the bathroom for her robe?

And then it hit me. I was with someone else's lover, not mine. I couldn't get out of "their" house fast enough. I phoned Will later and told him I felt like I was part of a threesome, and it didn't feel good. I mentioned his pronoun usage, the photos, and the necklace. He said he was sorry I felt that way, but he really liked his life the way it was. He thought the best thing for us to do was not to see each other.

And just like that, it was over.

DEANNE'S STORY

If you are dating a widower who cannot put his past relationships into his past, he is not ready to move forward. Being a widower does not give anyone the right to treat his current significant other as second best under any circumstances.

As a woman who dated and later married a widower, I expected to be treated as the most important woman in his life, just as I treated him as the most important man in my life. Does he think about his late wife periodically? I'm sure he does. Do I think about my ex-husband periodically? Absolutely. However, we both recognize that those relationships are *in the past*!

I cleared up any ambiguity with my husband early on in our relationship when we were spending one of our first holidays together. My husband (we were not married at the time) mentioned that he would be inviting his former in-laws (his late wife's family) over for the holiday because that had been their tradition. I responded that I would be inviting my former in-laws over for the holiday as well. He was quite surprised by my response, and he was not amused, but I got my point across very clearly. We decided that it was time for both of us to start new traditions! Since that time, I have always been consulted about who we would be sharing our time with.

6

SEX AND INTIMACY WITH A WIDOWER

EACH PERSON HAS THEIR OWN views about sex and when it's the right time to become intimate with another person. The purpose of this chapter is not to tell you when you should or shouldn't sleep with a widower—that's a personal decision you have to make. Rather, this chapter is about how widowed men think about and approach sex. This chapter will also provide some guidance if you want to avoid widowers who are just looking for casual hookups or a friends-with-benefits relationship.

Men and women think about sex differently. For example, back in Chapter 1, I discussed how men don't equate sex with commitment. I won't rehash that section here other than to say that women are more emotionally involved in a relationship when they have sex and tend to view sex as a way to up the commitment level. Men, on the other hand, tend to focus solely on the physical and pleasure aspects of sex. Even if you give a widower the best mind-blowing sex he's ever had, that won't make him love you more or take the relationship more seriously—it will just make him want more sex. The emotional attachment and commitment that come with sex will only happen *after* he's opened his heart to you.

Knowing how widowers think about and approach sex is important because women often assume that widowers who were in loving relationships with their late wife will take sex more seriously than single or divorced men. In reality, widowers tend to be more emotionally confused and conflicted after they have sex with someone other than their late wife. This is especially true if they had a long, monogamous marriage.

For example, some widowers feel sexually liberated when they start dating again. Their goal isn't to remarry or have a serious relationship, but to try to sleep with as many women as possible. Other widowers have a hard time performing in the bedroom because they feel guilty about sleeping with someone other than their late wife. Then there are widowers who have gone for years without sex with their late wife due to her illness or other factors. Often, these widowers are looking for someone to work out years of sexual frustration. There are widowers who don't believe in having sex until marriage and will wait to tie the knot before becoming sexually active. And yes, there are even widowers who fall somewhere in between and will take the time to get to know you and wait until you're both ready before becoming intimate.

So, how can you know if the widower is just using you for sex or is committed to a relationship with you? Here are three ways you can know his true feelings.

1. DON'T COMPROMISE YOUR SEXUAL STANDARDS

Everyone has different ideas about when it's appropriate to be sexually intimate with another person. Some don't mind sleeping with someone on a first date, while others will wait until marriage. Most people fall somewhere in between. What's important is that *you* know your standards and values regarding sex.

Throughout this book, I've talked about setting and maintaining healthy boundaries. Boundaries also apply to intimacy. Whatever your standards are, it's important that you hold firm to them, because whether or not a widower respects this boundary is a great indicator of what he thinks of you and your relationship. A widower seeking a long-term relationship won't pressure or force you to have sex before you're ready. He may test your standards to see how serious you are about keeping them, but he won't make you feel that you must have sex with him in order to move the relationship forward.

I have yet to talk with a woman who was glad she had sex with a widower *before* she was ready to do so. When the subject of sex comes up in a coaching session, it's usually because the woman felt pressured into sex before she was ready to take that step. Instead of feeling wanted or respected, these women feel used and manipulated—feelings that are made worse once the widower ends the relationship.

Julianna and I waited until we were married to have sex, and it was a value we both shared. But even if my sexual standards were different from hers, I still would have respected and accepted her boundaries. I cared about her and wanted the relationship to turn into something wonderful. Had I not cared about Julianna or was just looking for companionship or someone to sleep with, I might have pressured her to compromise her sexual standards. Knowing Julianna, she wouldn't have tolerated that behavior for very long and would have ended the relationship rather than giving in.

If you can't define what your values and standards are when it comes to sexual intimacy, you need to figure them out and hold firm to them. Otherwise, you're a prime target for widowers looking for short-term physical relationships who will dump you once they get bored.

2. TAKE YOUR TIME BEFORE BECOMING INTIMATE

It's okay to put off physical intimacy early in a relationship. In fact, the best way to sift out widowers who are looking for a fling is to take your time before having sex. The reason for this is simple: Widowers who are looking for a physical, short-term relationship won't be able to wait. Because their main goal is to sleep with you, they'll eventually become angry or frustrated when their sexual needs aren't met. Most of them will be patient for a short period of time, but the more sexually frustrated they become, the faster their true motives and desires will emerge.

Never give in to widowers' threats or demands for sex. If you feel pressured to have sex before you're ready or they're threatening to end the relationship unless you have sex, *don't give in*! End the relationship immediately. Their true colors and motives are showing. Giving in to his demands won't save the relationship or make him love you more. Once these widowers get whatever sexual fulfillment they want out of the relationship, they'll end it. All you'll have left is regret.

A widower who's interested in opening his heart to someone else will want that woman to feel comfortable and good about herself when they finally decide to become sexually intimate. He'll patiently wait until you're ready to take this step—even if it means waiting until marriage, if that's what you want.

Waiting to have sex also makes it easier to spot red flags. Becoming sexually intimate too quickly makes it easy to ignore the warning signs that he's not ready to open his heart. For example, it's easy to ignore the fact that he's not introducing you to friends or family when the sex is good. Or it's easy to rationalize away that he's still wearing a wedding ring or her photo is still in their bedroom when you think the physical intimacy means he cares about you.

By waiting to become intimate until we were married, Julianna was able to work through all the major widower-related concerns she had. She felt confident that I was ready to start a new chapter in my life with her. Waiting also gave me time to make sure I was ready to open my heart to her and put my life and marriage to Krista in a special place. That way, when we were ready to become physically intimate, we were both comfortable and confident with each other and the decision we made.

It's a decision neither of us regret.

3. THE LATE WIFE SHOULDN'T BE IN THE BEDROOM

When you finally decide to become intimate with a widower, one thing that shouldn't be around are images or reminders of the late wife. I bring this up because it seems like when women do become intimate with a widower, it's often in the same bed and the same room he and the late wife shared. While some women are okay with that, make sure photos of the late wife or her personal things aren't around. There's nothing worse than sharing an intimate moment with a widower, then spotting a photo of the late wife staring back at you, seeing her toiletries in the bathroom, or finding her clothes in the closet. Unless you're into threesomes, you need to talk to the widower about making his bedroom a place where you can feel comfortable.

For those who think asking the widower to remove his late wife's presence from the bedroom is a step too far, I have yet to coach a woman who enjoyed making love to a widower while the late wife looked on from the nightstand. His late wife didn't have to sleep with him while a photograph of his past girlfriend or ex-wife hung on the wall. Why should you be treated differently? If he's ready to open his heart, making you feel comfortable in the places where the two of you spend intimate moments shouldn't be a big deal.

Even though Julianna and I were married and living in a new apartment by the time we became intimate, she made it known that she had no desire to do anything in the same bed Krista and I shared. She wanted the bed and our bedroom to be something that was special to the two of us. The practical side of me was a little miffed, as there was nothing wrong with the bed from my marriage with Krista. Besides, Julie and I were young and poor. A new mattress was a big expense. Still, I knew that having a new bed was important to her and our marriage. When we returned from our honeymoon, the first thing we did was go out and buy a brand-new bed and mattress that served us well for many years.

Never settle for second place in the bedroom. If you do, don't be surprised when the widower treats you like second place elsewhere in his life. Widowers who want the sex between you to be special will wait until you're ready, then make whatever room you share a place where you will be comfortable. Whether that means clearing out all her things, replacing the mattress, or painting the walls, widowers who are ready to open their hearts will do what it takes to make these moments something you'll look forward to instead of regret.

KAREN'S STORY

My fiancé has never made comparisons between his late wife and me. He appreciates the fact that I am different, and he let me know that from day one. But early on, he wanted to share a couple stories about sex and the late wife. It was his way of showing that he was eager to do whatever he could to please me. Both times, I *shhhhed* him gently.

"What went on in Vegas should stay in Vegas, if you get my drift. I think your late wife would agree."

I don't talk about my bedroom history with anyone, period. Nor do I want to know anyone else's. This has been a personal policy I've always upheld out of respect for myself and for past lovers. Even my future husband doesn't get an exemption. A few times, his curiosity about my sexual past has led me to pull the "Don't ask, 'cause I'm not telling" card on him.

What's important is how you and I enjoy each other now, not what I used to do with someone else.

He nods and thanks me for the reminder.

CINDY'S STORY

"Bill" was widowed about a year before I met him. After his wife's death, he vowed not to make any changes in his life for a year, including not dating or changing anything in his house. But he was so miserably lonely and depressed after eleven months that one of his grown children convinced him to try a dating site.

Bill was sixty-six and I was sixty when we met online. Bill wasn't in the dating radius I wanted (he was two hundred miles away), but he was a nice-looking gentleman who otherwise fit my druthers (non-smoking, social drinking only, etc.). He was also a widower, so I thought perhaps he would be different from most of the divorced guys in my 50-60s age group who were narcissists or serial cheaters.

After a few messages online, we decided to move to telephone conversations. Within a few days, he told me he "had to come meet me before someone else snatched me up," so a week after our first text, he drove three hours on a weeknight to take me to dinner. We met at the restaurant, and it was simply magical, though I was trying hard to guard my heart. My recent dating experiences hadn't been great, so I was a bit gun-shy. Bill was obviously nervous, but we had a great conversation, and the chemistry was amazing. He walked me to my car, asked permission to give me a goodnight kiss, and we melted each other's hearts.

Fast forward a few months of dinner dates, morning-and-evening phone conversations, and one overnight stay at his house without intimacy. We were falling in love. He came to visit my town, and we stayed in a beautiful historic hotel. I think we both knew it was *the* night. Bill had been widowed more than a year by then. His late wife had been ill for several years prior to her death, and he had earlier confided they hadn't been intimate for several years before that. I hadn't been intimate with a man for about as long.

We were both nervous, and he was obviously feeling the pressure for everything to be perfect—romantic dinner, beautiful suite with wine, etc. In his nervousness, he had over-imbibed, but he wasn't drunk. However, at sixty-six, a guy on blood-pressure meds can't drink much and effectively be intimate. So, when we did go to bed, initially everything seemed fine, but as we got closer to having intercourse, he lost his erection and became very upset with himself for "disappointing" me. He was on the verge of tears. I pointed out that while alcohol increases desire, it doesn't help the male physiology, and I assured him that he could *never* disappoint me.

We snuggled and took a nap, then woke a bit later and had the most amazing experience I think either of us had ever had. We ended up making love, napping, and making love all night. Once that night, he called me his "lovely, lovely wife." I wasn't sure if he was projecting into the future or remembering the past, but he was so present with me that I let it go.

Bill says he'd never been a touchy-feely guy before he met me, but he couldn't stop holding me, and he said then (and several times since) that he'd had sex before, but now he knows what "making love" actually means. I believe in loving like you've never been hurt; Bill says I make him "feel like a man," and he hadn't felt that way in a long time.

We've been together more than a year now, and our life/love life just gets more amazing. But, as with most guys in their sixties, Bill occasionally has a slow night, or he thinks he can't perform. I've found that backing off, focusing on something else (conversation, nap, back rub) and then slowly working back into foreplay, giving him plenty of time to warm up, will almost always lead to an amazing night. I don't ever let my widower get upset with himself if he can't perform. I just redirect the energy to something else and enjoy our time together.

For the one-year anniversary of our first date, we took a vacation to a quaint historic town and had a wonderful time. On the last night of the trip, he proposed! Love (and great lovemaking) is still possible after a loss and at any stage of life. God's timing is perfect.

7

REMEMBERING THE LATE WIFE

YOU'LL EVENTUALLY ENCOUNTER DATES THAT are significant to your widower and his late wife.

The three big dates are the late wife's birthday, their wedding anniversary, and her date of death. There may be other special days, but for the purpose of this chapter, I'll focus on these three examples. The information in this chapter applies to any other occasions widowers deem significant.

When such a day approaches, you may be unsure what, if anything, you should do or say to support the widower you're dating. You may wonder if you should even acknowledge that day or if there's something you can say that will make it less painful. You find yourself in an awkward spot of wanting to be compassionate and understanding while simultaneously unsure whether you want to witness his emotional reaction. To make things worse, you may not even know what, if anything, he has planned for that day. If he does have plans to commemorate the date, you may struggle with deciding whether to go to the cemetery with him or attend a family event where everyone will talk about and remember the late wife.

There are no right or wrong answers to these situations. What you choose to do is a personal decision. This chapter will help you decide what's best for you and your relationship, how to cope with the roller coaster of emotions that accompany these days, and how to interpret a widower's behavior in order to recognize if any sort of commemoration on his part is helping him move forward or holding him back.

LET WIDOWERS ACKNOWLEDGE THESE DAYS IN THEIR OWN WAY

Each widower has his own way of observing days like the late wife's date of death. Some widowers visit the cemetery, while others post something on social media. I've known widowers to go to dinner with close friends and family members, while others just want some time alone. Aside from social media posts (which are a big no-no—more on that in a minute), there are no right or wrong ways for widowers to mark these days. Dealing with loss is unique to each person, and we all have our own ways of saying goodbye.

Never tell the widower what he can or can't do if he decides to acknowledge these days. If he wants to take flowers to the cemetery, don't stand in his way. If he wants to have a meal with family or other loved ones, let him do it. If he wants some quiet time alone, give it to him. If he wishes to do nothing and treat the day like any other, that's fine, too. This is his journey, and you need to let him take it. Marking these days, if done right, can actually help the widower move forward and want to open his heart.

After reading that last paragraph, some of you are wondering what healthy boundaries, if any, you can set on these special days, or if the widower should be allowed to do whatever he wants. There are three boundaries you should set that will make these days easier for you and the widower.

BOUNDARY #1: NO SOCIAL MEDIA POSTS

The first boundary is that the widower not post anything about his late wife on social media on that day. Chapter 8 talks in depth about social media usage and widowers, but for the purpose of this chapter, all you need to know is that publicly posting memories or photographs of the late wife and his loss encourages widowers to live in the past. We all get dopamine hits when someone likes or comments on one of our posts. All the likes that follow posts about the late wife and his loss subtly encourage the widower to live in the past. To be fair, those who comment on the posts probably don't mean to encourage that behavior, but that's the indirect effect of their actions.

If widowers choose to acknowledge the day, it needs to be done in a more private setting, either alone or with close friends and family. These more private events are more beneficial to the widower and can actually encourage him to move on.

BOUNDARY #2: YOU DON'T HAVE TO BE PART OF THE DAY

Whatever the widower wants to do, don't feel obligated to participate. For example, your widower may ask you if you'd like to visit the cemetery with him or attend a dinner with friends and family. Just like there's no right or wrong way for the widower to recognize these days, there's no right or wrong answer as to whether you should be part of these events. It's completely up to you.

Whatever you decide, you should spend some time thinking about it and then do what you feel is best. If you decide not to attend, don't sit around the house and wonder what the widower's doing or thinking. Instead, find something fun and positive to do. Go out with friends, participate in an activity you enjoy, or get out of town for the day. Just do something that can help you relax and take your mind off widower-related things so you'll be in a good mental state when you see him again.

If you do decide to participate, it's important that you go because you want to be there, not because you feel pressured to do so. These events are usually emotional for the widower, and if you're there out of a sense of obligation, it will make it an emotionally hard day for you and hurt your relationship in the long run.

To help you decide whether or not to attend, the widower should give you advance notice of his plans. If he doesn't know what he wants to do, that's fine, but don't let it stop you from making other plans for yourself. If anything, knowing that you already have something to do might spur him to make up his mind.

For some of you, telling the widower you don't want to participate in his plans may be difficult, but remember that this is an important boundary to set. Even if he is hurt by your decision not to be with him, he should respect it the same way you're allowing him to remember his late wife. You don't have to give the widower a detailed explanation of your decision. You can simply state that you don't feel comfortable attending, or say that it's something he should do on his own. What's important is that you do what is best for you in this situation.

BOUNDARY #3: THE WIDOWER SHOULD ONLY COMMEMORATE TWO OR THREE DAYS A YEAR

Some widowers want to integrate some sort of celebration of their late wives into every conceivable holiday or special occasion. This is unacceptable behavior for a widower in a serious relationship. Instead, he should pick two or three days a year to acknowledge the late wife.

Widowers who resist placing limits on the number of days to visit the cemetery or commiserate with family and friends aren't completely ready to move forward. If you need to set a boundary, let him pick the days he wants. It's not important which days or events he wants to acknowledge, but rather, that he picks the ones that mean the most to him. Anything more than three would indicate that he's not ready to live in the present and focus on the future.

For those who are wondering how long widowers will want to acknowledge certain days, know that the desire to remember the late wife is most intense in the first three years after loss. The want or need to acknowledge these days fades as the years go by and as new relationships grow stronger. While the widower may pick three days this year, odds are that in a few years, it will be down to one or even zero days.

For those who are worried that doing something to commemorate those days will draw him back to the past or hurt your relationship, pay attention to how he's doing emotionally in the days following. If the widower is acting like his normal self, that's a sign that he's dealing with his loss in a healthy way. If he becomes depressed, moody, angry, or is verbally or emotionally abusive after these events, that's a sign that the way he's choosing to remember the late wife isn't good for either his emotional health or your relationship.

In an email, one woman told me that her widower went to the cemetery once a week. She dreaded those days because he always came home in a nasty mood that lasted for two or three days after. I told her that this behavior was not acceptable and that he either needed to stop these visits or she needed to take a step back from the relationship. I'm glad to report that after she drew healthy boundaries, the widower drastically reduced the number of cemetery visits and their relationship improved.

HOW I ACKNOWLEDGE SPECIAL DAYS

The first year after Krista's death, I visited the gravesite shared by her and my daughter, Hope, at least once a week. Most of the time, I went by myself so I could have some time and space to think about things. When I started dating Julianna, the frequency of these visits decreased to every other week. By the time Julianna and I became exclusive, they were even more infrequent.

The only time Julianna accompanied me to the cemetery was on the first anniversary of Krista's death. I let Julianna know that she didn't have to come with me, but she told me it was something that she wanted to be part of. The full details of this day can be found in the last chapter of my memoir, *Room for Two*. When I visited the gravesite that day, I said my final goodbyes to Krista.

On the drive home, I resolved *not* to visit the cemetery or publicly acknowledge or commemorate dates that were important to me and Krista. I wanted my full emotional attention to be on Julianna and our soon-to-be marriage. The last thing I wanted to do was participate in an activity that might set me back emotionally or hurt our relationship. As of the time I write this, it's been seventeen years since I last visited Krista and Hope's grave.

I have no regrets about that decision.

I don't recommend that all widowers follow this course of action. If my daughter Hope had lived, I probably would make occasional visits to the cemetery with her. Graveside visits are probably something I would have continued if Julianna hadn't come along.

Even Julianna thought it was odd that I didn't want to visit the cemetery at all. A few months after we were married, Memorial Day weekend arrived, and Julianna asked if I was planning on visiting the cemetery. I remember feeling puzzled because I had told her that I had no intention to visit Krista's grave again. I told her that I wanted to spend the weekend with her. She asked me if I was sure about that, because she wanted me to know that she would support my decision to visit Krista and Hope if it was something I wanted to do.

Julianna and I repeated this conversation several times in the first three years or so of our marriage. Eventually, she stopped bringing it up. Even though I never took her up on her offers, I appreciated that she left that option open for me. This hasn't been a topic of conversation in over a decade, but I know that if I ever wanted to visit Krista and Hope's grave, Julianna would support my decision.

AMY'S STORY

The widower I'm dating has two children, ages three and seven. We have been dating for 11 months, and I see his kids two or three times a week. My relationship with the kids started early on while we were dating. I felt so sad they didn't have a mother, and I would go in their rooms and read to them or just talk.

With the seven-year-old, I would touch base with her every few weeks and ask her how she was doing. She discussed things with me that she didn't necessarily discuss with her dad. She and I started bonding pretty early on. There were times, on more than one occasion, when I had to excuse myself from the room because my eyes were filled with tears. One of those times, the seven-year-old said she wanted a life-sized cutout of her mother so she could hug it all the time. Another time, I was rocking the then two-year-old and singing to him, and the tears started because I was just thinking that his mom should have been the one holding him and loving on him.

The widower and I plan on getting married this year, but we are not in the same house now, so I do not yet have the "mom" role. I do recall a painful comment by the seven-year-old while we were out to dinner. A child thought I was her mom and said a comment to her about it. She said, "Why does everyone think you are my mom? I hate it when people do that." I don't know if this came about because I am, in fact, not her mom, or if she is scared to allow someone else to have that title besides her real mother. Her dad spoke with her, letting her know it is okay that she has another mom. He explained to his daughter that her mother is never coming back physically. He told her he knows how much she wants her mom back, but no matter what, she won't be back here on Earth.

My hopes are that one day, she and her brother do accept me as their mother. I don't want them to ever forget their mother, and I want them to learn about her. At the same time, I want them to have a living mother who can love them unconditionally, hug them, nurture them, and help raise them.

CAROLYN'S STORY

After ten years of being a divorcée and working my way unsuccessfully through Match.com and other dating websites, I decided to give up looking and just have fun. That was when my next-door neighbor asked me to let his father run around with me to dance classes, plays, and bluegrass concerts.

The first time we had dinner, he informed me that we were not "dating." I responded, "Of course not, we are just hanging out together." After seven occasions of "hanging out," he kissed me. I advised him that I didn't kiss my hanging-out friends in that manner. He said that he had changed his mind and wanted to date me. After four months of dating, he told me that he hoped that I was not expecting marriage, as he had no intentions of ever marrying again. I told him that I was living in the present and not the future—therefore, I was taking it one day at a time and had no expectations. Once upon a time, I wanted to remarry and was actively seeking a spouse. I now know that until my W gets further along in his grieving process, he is not marriageable material.

Since I am the first woman he seriously dated after the death of his wife, I suggested that he might want to date other women. He didn't like that idea and asked me to just be patient with him.

I have discovered that dating a widower is very different than dating a divorced man. Choices have to be made regarding what you will tolerate (jewelry, constant talk about his wife, comparisons, and lots of mementoes of his late wife) and how long you will tolerate them. Divorced men don't have as much of a problem telling you that they love you, as they don't feel as if they are being disloyal to anyone.

Some days, it was very hard when he told my friends and family about things he and his late wife did together. They looked embarrassed for me. I finally realized that his nearly five decades with his LW was the only point of reference he had when meeting new people. He and I have been slowly building experiences together, and the mentions of his LW have slowed down considerably.

Would I date a widower again? Absolutely. My widower has all the qualities of a significant other that I have always wanted. He is well worth being around and having patience that things will change. The bottom line when dating a widower is that you must have patience for him to work through his grieving process. Things do change, although it will not be as quick as most women would want.

8

WIDOWERS AND SOCIAL MEDIA

SOCIAL MEDIA IS THE GATEWAY to the soul. If you want to know what someone really thinks, values, and believes, just look through their social media accounts. In minutes, you'll discover the causes they champion and the people they love. When it comes to widowers, seeing what photos they post and stories they share can give you incredible insight into how far along they are on their grief journey and whether they're ready to open their hearts.

In widower relationships, social media is also a huge source of stress. From widowers and their friends sharing photos and memories of the late wives to widowers refusing to update their profile pictures, there's a unique set of issues to overcome if the relationship has any chance of success.

SHOULD WIDOWERS REMEMBER THE LATE WIFE ON SOCIAL MEDIA?

In the previous chapter, we discussed healthy ways widowers can remember their late wives, if they so choose. Options include graveside visits, meals with family, or time alone. Instead of these options, many widowers want to remember their late wives on social media. This includes sharing pictures, posting about how much they miss their late wives, and acknowledging dates like wedding anniversaries or dates of death.

When widowers share memories about their late wives in such a public manner, it makes the women they're dating wonder if the widowers are ready to open their hearts. It's a valid concern, because sharing those thoughts and memories with the world could indicate that the widowers aren't ready.

Widowers who are in serious relationships shouldn't share photos or memories about their late wives on social media.

Period.

If widowers post anything about love or relationships, it should be about their current relationship and the memories they're making now—not good times and recollections about the past. If you're in an exclusive relationship with a widower and he's posting about the late wife, you need to ask him to stop. This is a healthy but firm boundary you need to set with him to protect your sanity and to strengthen your relationship.

For those who are wondering why I support the occasional cemetery visit or family get-togethers but not social media posts, here's the reason: Gravesite visits or spending time with friends and family are more personal, sincere expressions of grief and loss. If done right, these moments can be very helpful in saying goodbye to the late wife and moving forward with a new love. On the other hand, social media is fueled by the dopamine hits that come from likes and comments. The more something is liked or commented on, the bigger rush people get, and the more likely they are to post about such things in the future. When a widower gets a positive reaction to posts about the late wife, it *encourages* him to stay focused on the past and his loss instead of the wonderful relationship he has now.

For example, let's say a widower posts a wedding photo to commemorate what would have been their twenty-fifth wedding anniversary. In response, his social media post is flooded with likes and comments from friends and family about how much they miss the late wife, what a great marriage they had together, and how they're thinking about him on this special day. All these reactions subtly encourage him to post more. (To be fair, I don't think those who like, comment on, or share the widower's social media posts are doing so with the intention of holding him back from falling in love again. They're doing what they think is supportive and helpful—even though it has the opposite effect.)

No relationship can survive when one or both parties are talking publicly about how much they miss a past love. If a single or divorced man was pining on social media about a former girlfriend or ex-wife, most people would realize that he wasn't ready to open his heart to someone else. Yet when it comes to widowers, a different standard is not only applied, but it's often encouraged.

When you set healthy boundaries with widowers about social media activity, keep in mind that they may not know these posts upset you or that it's hurting your relationship. They may be doing it out of habit or because they feel sharing memories of the late wife is expected of them. And they probably don't realize how the positive reactions to such posts subtly encourage them to dwell in the past. When you talk to them about this topic, give them the benefit of the doubt. A widower who sees a future with you will respect these boundaries and adjust his behavior accordingly. It only becomes a red flag and relationship poison if he keeps posting after you've asked him to stop.

HOW TO HANDLE SOCIAL MEDIA TORCHBEARERS

A widower's friends and family may also post tributes and photographs of his late wife. Even if you aren't connected to them on social media, they'll tag the widower, which means you will see the posts in your social media feed whether you want to or not. To make matters worse, their posts aren't always to remember a special occasion like the late wife's birthday, so they can pop up unexpectedly.

Friends and family who constantly post about the late wife are referred to as torchbearers. Their main objective is to keep the memory of the late wife alive. If you find that torchbearers are ruining your social media experience, there's a simple solution: take control of your social media feed. You have the power to unfollow, block, or unfriend those who are constantly posting things about the late wife. As part of this, widowers should update their social media settings so their torchbearing friends and family can't tag them in posts and photos without their approval.

Don't let the social media habits of others come between you and the widower. If others want to live in the past, that's their business. You have no control over what others think or post online. You do have the ability not to let those actions ruin your relationship, especially when you have power over what you see and who you interact with on social media. Social media is what you allow it to be.

SHOULD THE WIDOWER DELETE PHOTOS OF THE LATE WIFE?

Most social media platforms store posts and photos unless they're deleted by the user. As a result, widowers often have large caches of photos and memories stored as part of their accounts. The question is sometimes asked whether widowers should delete these posts and photos, especially if they make the new girlfriend uncomfortable.

The answer is no.

Everyone has a past, and asking a widower to delete a bunch of pictures is akin to asking him to erase that past. Photos and other memories of the late wife should be deleted *only* if the widower spends a lot of time looking at them or shares these past memories on social media.

The good news is that most widowers don't spend time scrolling through past photos on their social media. More often, it's their new girlfriend who spends time scrolling through them.

My advice to live in the present and focus on the future also applies to those who date widowers. This means you shouldn't spend time looking at the widower's past photos and posts about the late wife on his social media account. I know there's a curiosity factor about her and the life she and the widower shared together in order to better understand the man you're dating. However, this type of activity usually results in either jealousy or thoughts that you'll never measure up to her.

You aren't in a competition. She's dead and isn't coming back. The widower has chosen to start a new chapter of his life with someone else. If you want that person to be you, spend your time making new memories with the widower—memories he'll want to share with those he's connected to on social media. Leave the past where it belongs, and spend that time strengthening your relationship and creating memories that will last a lifetime.

THE LATE WIFE'S SOCIAL MEDIA ACCOUNTS

Sometimes, the late wife's social media accounts are still active, and the widower takes a role in managing her account. This is not healthy for him, you, or your relationship. Ideally, the social media account should either be memorialized (if that's an option) or put into some sort of state where others can view it, but not interact with it. Deleting the account is a last resort and should only be done if there's no other option or if the widower is spending too much time looking at it. Avoid dating widowers who don't want to give up control of the late wife's accounts. If you do, you'll always live in her electronic shadow.

UPDATING YOUR RELATIONSHIP STATUS

Some social media platforms like Facebook allow users to post their relationship status. Sometimes widowers don't update their status, and they still show themselves as either widowers or married to the late wife. Status should be updated when they are in an exclusive relationship and ready to share that with the world.

If he hasn't changed his status, this isn't necessarily a red flag. If he's not a big social media user, that's one thing, and a little nudging can get him to update his profile. However, if the widower doesn't want to update it because of what others might think or say, that's a red flag. Though not everyone may support his new relationship, letting the thoughts and reactions of others dictate the terms of your relationship is never a good sign. Widowers who deem the thoughts of others more important than yours will never make you the center of their hearts.

Remember that social media is an insightful way to know what direction widowers' hearts are pointed. If his heart is turned to the late wife, give him one chance to make you number one.

Talking to the widower about his social media behavior and setting healthy boundaries can be difficult, but learning how to communicate with each other is vital to the success of your relationship. If you can't learn how to talk to each other, your relationship won't survive. And if you aren't sure how to talk to him, my next chapter covers that very subject.

RACHEL'S STORY

Social media can cause so much pain. I don't believe people are intentionally trying to cause pain, but they don't think before they post.

It's been five years since the late wife passed away, and over four years that my husband and I have been together. This summer, my brother-in-law, who I get along with, posted a picture on Facebook of the late wife, my husband, his sister, and himself and tagged everyone in it.

Thankfully, I have not had to deal with too many of these kinds of posts, but this one hit hard. My husband commented with a sad face, thanked him for sharing, and said how it seemed like a lifetime ago.

While I do understand the pain of losing a loved one, I don't think others understand what these posts do to our family unit as it looks now. It hurts me, and it hurts my husband, and it sometimes hurts our relationship.

A lot of marriages end in divorce. Relationships end for many reasons, and family members who once loved that person move on without posting comments or pictures about the ex-spouse/significant other. Yet that same discretion seems to go out the window in this situation. It's a constant reminder of being caught in the shadow of what was once his life and being in his life because of his loss.

I don't often say something to my husband about these things because I always end up the bad guy when he tries to defend me or my views to his or the late wife's family. But I still see it, and I still feel it.

PATTIE'S STORY

We went to school together in a small community. I was a year older, and our circles never really crossed. We knew each other, but never had a friendship. He met his late wife in high school. We went our separate ways without a thought. Fast forward over ten years. His late wife passed away after a long battle with cancer. She was a fighter. He fought just as hard. In the end, her body was tired.

Due to our jobs, his in law enforcement and mine in child protective services, we bumped into each other. It's unexplainable, and we did not talk about it at first, but later on, we discovered we both felt the presence of something strong. Fast forward a bit—he got the courage to message me on social media. We talked briefly about getting together for lunch. We ended up meeting up shortly after and instantly hit it off.

I tried to go into the relationship understanding that he was in pain and going through a process I would never understand, but could support him in. Fast forward a couple more months—in an irrational moment, he posted about our relationship on social media. Some were happy for us, some were not. It caused an uproar that was heard around our tiny community. Opinions and accusations and investigations of timelines flew throughout. I had people coming up to me in professional settings, asking me questions about our relationship. It was hard on me, him, and us.

On top of it all, I was in the process of being a surrogate. I warned him before our relationship got a start.

He was completely supportive of the choice. But by the time our relationship went public, I had a bump, and again, everyone starting doing the math. It hurt my heart for him and the respect I have for his late wife. He wouldn't do such a thing, and neither would I.

The chaos has mostly calmed down. There is no communication between me and the late wife's family. I believe in my heart that will change one day.

Social media has been a hardship. His wife's battle with cancer was very public, as was her passing. His grieving process has been public, too. I have tried to respect him, but at times, social media can be a jab to the side. His feelings for me do not appear on social media, but his love for his wife and his life away from me do. I am working on this daily. We are six months into our relationship. We grow stronger every day. There are setbacks, but with Abel's guidance, I have learned so much about my feelings and my widower's, and how communication and boundaries are the keys to a successful relationship.

9

HOW TO TALK TO A WIDOWER

THROUGHOUT THIS BOOK, I'VE STRESSED the importance of learning to communicate so you can discuss widower issues, your needs, and healthy boundaries. For many people, however, the mere thought of having these conversations is stressful. This chapter is dedicated specifically to five communications strategies that will help you talk with your widower. When you know how men like to communicate, you can tailor your words so he'll listen to you, and your conversation will have the best chance of success.

COMMUNICATION STRATEGY #1: MEN LIKE TO SOLVE PROBLEMS

The first thing you need to know about men—widowed or otherwise—is that they're natural problem-solvers. That means when you talk to them about a relationship issue, they automatically go into problem-solving mode. While you're talking, most men are figuring out how to solve it—assuming they think it's a problem that needs to be fixed. You can use this to your advantage when talking about relationship concerns.

The first thing you want to do is get straight to the point. Men are in a constant state of anxiety until you tell them the reason for the conversation. Their desire to fix things makes it hard to sit and listen for more than a few minutes—especially if they think they already have an answer. Don't go into details. Just tell him what's on your mind as succinctly as possible.

Next, instead of telling the widower how to solve the problem, explain how the issue makes you feel and hurts your relationship. Unless it's put into this context, widowers will see the issue as "your problem" and not something that affects them. When they see that the issue could have serious consequences for their love life, it makes them more invested in finding a solution. It also forces them to take the important but necessary step of deciding what they value more: you or the status quo.

Finally, give widowers an opportunity to figure out their own solutions. I recommend this approach, because one of the ways men express their love is through sacrifice and action. As a result, they become more invested in you and in the relationship. It also increases the odds that they're fixing things because they *want* to do it rather than because you asked them to do it.

When widowers do something just to placate the women they're dating, it makes them resentful and will eventually come back to bite you the next time you have an argument. For example, I've talked with women who told the widower to take down pictures of the late wife instead of explaining to him how the photographs made her think he wasn't ready to move forward. While the widower removed the photos to pacify her, the very next time they had an argument, he threw her request in her face by putting the photographs back up or telling her that he only did it because she asked him to—not because he wanted to do it.

So, how do you have such a conversation? Here's an example. Say the urn containing the late wife's ashes is on the mantel. The fact that they're in such a prominent place makes you uncomfortable every time you're at the widower's home and makes you feel like he isn't ready to open his heart. You want him to either move the urn to a less visible location or to scatter the ashes, but you know that he needs to come up with a solution. A good way to talk about the issue would be something like this:

> **You:** We need to talk about the urn on the mantel.
>
> **Widower:** Okay, what about it?
>
> **You:** When we were snuggling on the couch last night, it was hard for me to enjoy our time together because I kept looking at it. I know the urn is important to you, but every time I see it, it makes me feel like you're not ready to open your heart.
>
> **Widower:** What do you want me to do about it?

You: That's up to you. I'm just letting you know how it makes me feel, and that it affects our relationship. I love you and want this relationship to work, but it's hard for me to open my heart to you when I see the urn sitting on the mantel.

While your actual conversation may not be as succinct as this one, take note of how quickly it got to the point and how the problem was explained in terms of affecting the relationship. No one beat around the bush or gave unnecessary details. If your conversation went something along these lines, most widowers would understand your thoughts and feelings about the urn and know that something needs to be done. They may not have a solution at that exact moment, but they're thinking about where it could be moved or wondering if it's a good time to scatter her ashes.

Sometimes, widowers will push back and say something like, "What do you want me to do?" If he says that, put the solution back on him. Don't make the decision for him. When widowers must decide, they're forced to determine if they value the relationship enough to solve the problem. It's an internal struggle that all widowers must go through if they're going to open their hearts to someone else.

The only time you should tell him what to do is when it comes to addictive or abusive behaviors. For example, if the widower is an alcoholic, simply telling him that his drinking is ruining the relationship isn't enough. You need to tell him to stop drinking and seek help or the relationship will come to an end. If he doesn't act, end the relationship immediately.

COMMUNICATION STRATEGY #2: DON'T ACT JEALOUS

If you want any chance of the widower listening to your concerns and solving the problem, do not come across as jealous of the late wife. If you feel jealous, that's okay. Everyone who has dated a widower has been jealous of the late wife at one time or another. It's hard not to feel that way about someone who's portrayed as a saint. But no matter how jealous you may be, you need to keep the conversation focused on you, the widower, and your relationship. If the widower thinks your comments are motivated by something other than love, he won't listen to anything you have to say.

Going back to the urn scenario, here's an example of what *not* to say:

> **You:** Every time I'm at your house, I feel like your wife is watching us. Why won't you scatter her ashes or put the urn someplace where I don't have to see it? I feel like you can't say goodbye to her and aren't ready to move on.

In the above example, the focus is on the late wife and the widower's marriage instead of your relationship. Even if everything in the above example is true, widowers interpret those comments as an attack on the late wife. A better approach is one that acknowledges his feelings for the late wife while focusing on your relationship and the future.

An example of how to say things that way goes something like this:

You: When I come over to your house, I don't feel completely comfortable because all I can see and think about is the urn. I know the urn is important to you, and I understand why you have it on the mantel. If it were my spouse who had passed on, I'd probably do something similar. However, the fact that you haven't scattered her ashes yet makes me feel like you aren't ready for a serious relationship.

See the difference? In the second example, the focus is on how the urn impacts you, his ability to move forward, and his current relationship instead of his late wife. When you make it about the two of you, widowers are more receptive to your concern.

Julianna was great at keeping conversations focused on us and our future instead of the past. I don't remember her coming across as jealous of Krista when we talked (even though she was at times). For example, I sometimes accidentally called Julianna "Krista." When we talked about it, the conversation focused on what was going through my mind, whether I was ready to move on, and how those slips of the tongue made Julianna feel. I never felt that Julianna was attacking Krista or my marriage to her. Instead, all I felt from her was loving concern about our relationship and our future together.

COMMUNICATION STRATEGY #3: DISCUSS ONE ISSUE AT A TIME

Often, there's not just one widower-related issue, but several issues that need to be resolved. In order to have the best chance of success, address one issue and work on solving that. Men are much better at listening and being receptive when they tackle one problem at a time. For example, let's say the widower you're dating still wears his wedding ring, has a shrine to the late wife in the main room of the house, and hasn't told his kids about you. If you bring up all three issues in one conversation, you're going to overwhelm him, and he will either tune you out or think that you're nagging or complaining. Instead, pick one issue—ideally the fastest and easiest one—and work on that.

If the widower can successfully change a small thing, it teaches him that it's possible to make even more complex changes. It also teaches the two of you how to work through an easy issue before tackling more difficult problems. Besides, if the widower isn't willing to make a small, easier change, he's never going to make the more difficult ones.

Julianna faced several issues when we first started dating—I wore my wedding ring on a chain around my neck, I had photos of the late wife all over my house, and I referred to Krista as my wife. To Julianna's credit, she didn't let all these issues overwhelm her. Instead, she went about discussing and resolving them with me one at a time. The first thing we talked about was me calling Krista my wife. Next, we moved on to the wedding ring, and finally, the photos in the home. By the time we got engaged seven months after our first date, all of these problems were resolved, and we both felt comfortable moving forward. Working on these issues taught us how to communicate and resolve problems together—a pattern we continue to follow to this day. If Julie had brought up all three concerns in the same conversation, I wouldn't have been as receptive to her, and there's a chance it may have ended the relationship before it had a chance to get off the ground.

You know what you can and can't live with. No matter how many widower-related issues need to be addressed, prioritize them and work on them one at a time. A widower who is ready to open his heart will work to resolve your concerns.

COMMUNICATION TIP #4: FOCUS ON PROBLEMS THE WIDOWER CAN ACTUALLY SOLVE

There are going to be some widower-related issues you need to deal with on your own. For example, some women struggle with the fact that a small portion of the widower's heart will always belong to the late wife. It's a valid concern, but one the widower can't fix for you. This doesn't mean you can't tell him about it, but if you do, let him know that you don't expect him to solve it.

After Julianna and I started discussing marriage, she told me there were times when it was difficult for her to want to spend the rest of her life with me. She then explained that there were things that would be firsts for her (marriage, buying a house, and starting a family) but were going to be seconds for me. While she was talking, my mind was spinning. It was impossible for me to make her the first person I married or started a family with. What did she expect me to do about it? It wasn't until the end of the conversation that she admitted these were internal issues that only she could solve. At that point, I finally began to relax. Occasionally, she'd update me on how she was doing and tell me again that they were her own issues and that she appreciated me listening to her. It's a technique she's perfected over the years that makes communication better for both of us.

TIP #5: WIDOWERS HAVE TO RE-LEARN TO COMMUNICATE

Unless you're a clone of the late wife, you probably have a different background, style, and tastes. You probably have a different love language and communication style than she did. As a result, one of the challenges widowers face is learning how to listen and talk to you instead of the late wife. This is a difficult but not impossible transition.

For example, my late wife, Krista, had a very outgoing personality. She wasn't afraid to tell me what was on her mind or what she thought about things. Though I always knew what she thought, often her style meant that we ended up arguing about things instead of talking them out. Julianna's personality and communication style are the opposite of Krista's. She is on the quiet side and typically takes her time thinking about things before talking about them.

As a result, when Julianna and I were first together, I would find myself creating an argument simply because that's how Krista and I worked through our issues. But that wasn't Julie's style, and as a result, it caused a lot of problems when we were dating and first married. Thankfully, we learned how to communicate better over the sixteen years we've been married, and though we still have the occasional communication snafu, they are few and far between.

Learning to communicate with each other is something widowers and the women dating them need to work on continually. The conversations you have with a widower aren't going to be smooth and perfect. What's important is that you both work to understand how to communicate with each other. These five tips won't solve all your communication issues, but they will help you both avoid big pitfalls and increase the chance for long-term relationship success.

TAMI'S STORY

It was important for me to have an open door communication policy with my widower. I made it clear from the start that in order for any relationship to work, communication had to be the key. We both made it possible for it to be successful by telling one another about our desires, what made us happy, what made us mad, and what things we looked for in a significant other. My widower had been without his late wife for only six weeks when we started our whirlwind romance. Her death was still fresh, and he was numb. Each day we spent together made it harder for me to understand what he was truly feeling. Most of the time, we were doing normal things you do when you first starting dating someone (movies, dinner, concerts, etc.).

After I started to develop stronger feelings, I told him where my heart and mind were. I asked him how he was progressing and if he saw a future for us. At that time, he said he was still in love with her. It was hard being in love with him and not having those feelings reciprocated towards me but to a woman who died. I wondered if he would ever fall in love with me. He had to reassure me of his thoughts and feelings often. Once, I asked him if he had never met her but had met me instead, could he see himself falling in love with me? When he answered, "yes," I knew that all I had to do was wait. He had to make the transition from being in love with her for the rest of his life, to loving someone else and possibly falling in love again. He had to be determined to make room for a new love; that's not something I could do for him.

The most important lesson I learned was to be open and patient. I had to be open to the idea that he may or may not fall in love with me, and I had to be patient for him to come to those realizations on his own. He had to decide whether he was ready or not—there was nothing I could have done to change that. It wasn't about me making him happy, but it was about him finding happiness within himself again. As it turns out, he did fall in love with me, and we are moving forward each and every day. If he had not fallen in love with me, I would have been hurt, but you can't force love on people, widower or not. It has to be mutual.

LESLEIGH'S STORY

I am now engaged to a wonderful widower with whom I'm very much in love. It has been a three-year road of being extremely patient, seeking my own counsel in psychotherapy, and continuing to let go of the expectation that my sweetheart's only child, a lovely, young 21-year-old woman, would accept me as someone other than her father's (then) girlfriend and now fiancée.

At the beginning of our relationship, Bryan's daughter, Britney, appeared to be happy that her father was dating, not alone, and having some fun again. She was 16 when her mother was diagnosed with cancer and had the horrific responsibility of sometimes even driving her mom to chemotherapy treatments.

When her father and I became closer, it was very difficult for Britney to accept me in her father's life. Perhaps she would have had an easier time if I hadn't been the first woman that he dated after his late wife passed away. Our relationship was difficult for Britney, and soon I realized that her lack of acceptance had *nothing* to do with me and everything to do with her healing process.

Last year, Britney graduated from college but struggled with inviting me to her graduation because she was so sad that her mom wasn't alive to attend with her father. I didn't go to the graduation. Bryan wanted me by his side, and I wanted to be with him, but it was more important to support his daughter's wishes. This was *her* special event. I had to grow another emotional skin once again.

When Bryan and I became engaged, I received a text from his daughter a few days later saying, "Congratulations!" It didn't make her wrong for not picking up the phone; I understand that she is doing the best she can to add me into the mix of her life. It has tremendously helped this past year that *she* has an important new man in her own life and doesn't have the need to lean so much on her dad.

I don't expect that Britney and I will be close friends soon. I give her space, and I am respectful. We don't use the word "love," and I accept that she holds me at a distance. It's okay. She is happy that her father is happy now, and we have moved many steps closer in our communication over these three years. My advice to anyone dating a widower with an adult child is to realize that whatever behaviors seem distancing by his adult child/children are not meant personally. Their attitude has a lot to do with simply trying to make sense of their own loss and trying to move ahead in their own life as best as she/he can.

10

WHAT TO DO IF YOUR RELATIONSHIP WITH A WIDOWER ENDS

NOT EVERY RELATIONSHIP WITH A widower has a happy ending. Roughly 70% of widower relationships end within a year after the first date. Though breakups can be heart-wrenching, the purpose of dating is to get to know each other and decide if you're a long-term fit. Not everyone is. It's better to find out if you're compatible as quickly as possible instead of wasting years of your life with someone who can't return your love and give you the kind of relationship you want.

It's my hope that your relationship with a widower becomes something better, stronger, and more wonderful than you both ever imagined. In case it doesn't, however, this chapter helps you understand why widowers end relationships and how to avoid the mistakes that prolong heartbreak and make it difficult for you to move forward.

WHY WIDOWERS END RELATIONSHIPS

When widowers call off relationships, it usually comes as a surprise to their girlfriends who were under the impression that things were not perfect, but slowly moving forward. No breakup is easy, but they're even more devastating when they catch you off guard.

Widowers will give you various reasons for ending the relationship. Common excuses include: they're still grieving, their kids don't want them in a serious relationship, or they're simply not ready to open their hearts. No matter their explanation, widowers end relationships for one of two reasons:

1. The relationship became too serious, and the widower realized he was never fully committed to you.

2. The widower grew tired or bored of the relationship and is looking for someone new to date.

Some of you are reading this and trying to square the excuse(s) your widower gave you with one or both reasons above. To help you better understand how widowers think, here are two examples that will help clarify their thought process when ending a relationship.

In the first example, you and the widower have what seems like a great relationship. Things aren't perfect, but he appears to be making progress, and the relationship is moving forward. The two of you have just taken a fabulous trip or spent a fun weekend together. During this time, things were going so well that the two of you discussed taking the relationship to the next level. This may have included meeting his and/or your family or kids, moving in together, or marriage. In the days following this trip or weekend, you were thrilled that things were finally getting serious.

Then, out of the blue, the widower ends the relationship. Reasons for the breakup—assuming he can even give you one—are that he started dating too soon, he's still grieving, or he's still in love with his late wife. The news takes you completely by surprise. You just had a great time together, and things were finally becoming serious. How could he bring things to such an abrupt end?

Despite outward appearances, the widower was never into the relationship as much as both of you thought. The relationship gave him a reason to get up in the morning. It served as a distraction from his grief, sorrow, and loss. He enjoyed spending time together, and for the first time since his wife died, he was happy again.

Then came the talk about meeting his or your family, moving in together, or getting married. While the widower was enthusiastic at the time, the conversation forced him to evaluate how invested he really was in a future with you. After some soul-searching, he realized that his heart wasn't into the relationship as much as he thought or led you to believe. The result is an unexpected and devastating breakup.

In the second example, your relationship started out great, but eventually plateaued and has been in a holding pattern for some time. You've done everything you can to show the widower that you're ready for a more serious, committed relationship, but have been met with excuse after excuse as to why he's not ready. The widower asks for your patience so he can make room in his heart for you. You give him the time and space he asks for and wait for him to work through his issues.

Then the relationship ends. The breakup isn't necessarily unexpected. Before the breakup, there was some tension between the two of you that built up over time, or maybe you told him to make up his mind. Whatever issues preceded the breakup, the widower gives you a laundry list of excuses as to why he's not ready to open his heart.

The more shocking part isn't the breakup itself. It's that within days or weeks of it ending, you discover he's back in the dating game. Maybe he's dating someone else or has reactivated his profile on an online dating site. You wonder how he could be dating again so soon after telling you he wasn't ready to open his heart.

One of two things happened that triggered the breakup. Either the widower grew bored of the relationship and ended things because he was ready to find someone else, or he was happy with how things were and had no plans to change, only to become irritated when you asked him to step up and make you a priority in his life. In the latter, he's decided that he's better off finding someone who will tolerate the fact that he hasn't and won't move on with his life.

In either scenario, within days or weeks following the breakup, the widower is likely back on dating sites and is soon with someone else. He's not interested in or looking for a long-term, committed relationship. Rather, he's just looking for a warm body to take the place of his late wife.

YOU DID NOTHING WRONG

Often after a widower relationship ends, the woman wonders if she could have said or done something that would have prevented the breakup. The truth is, there's nothing that would have stopped the relationship from ending. Starting a new chapter is something widowers have to want and be motivated to do. A relationship can be a reason for moving forward, but his grief is something internal that he must work through.

YOU CAN'T DO ANYTHING TO CHANGE HIS MIND

For those who are wondering if there's anything you can do or say that will help a widower change his mind, there isn't. When men end relationships, they've already moved on. Most of them moved on mentally before they actually ended the relationship. They're also not wondering how you're feeling, or agonizing about whether they made the right decision. I share this in case you're tempted to reach out to a widower to get an explanation or a reason for the breakup. Though some widowers will respond to a text or an email, most won't. And those who do usually won't give you a satisfactory answer. The best thing you can do is focus on you and putting your life back together instead of wondering what went wrong. And even if they do give you an answer, all it does is make the breakup worse.

For example, when I ended my relationship with Jennifer, she was devastated. It was out of the blue, and the last thing she expected when I called her up. A few days after I ended things, she sent me an email asking me to explain my actions. My gut told me to ignore the email or just write a short reply saying that it was over. Instead, I did my best to explain things to her. It ended up being a mistake, because a few days later, a mutual friend reached out and said that my email had made things worse for Jennifer and given her more things to agonize over. She read so much into my explanation that she spent the next several months waiting for me to come to my senses and change my mind—something that simply wasn't going to happen.

SHOULD YOU GIVE WIDOWERS A SECOND CHANCE?

After a breakup, some widowers will ask for a second chance. This usually comes with an admission that he made a mistake, a lengthy apology, and a promise that things will be different once you're back together. This may sound like a tempting offer, and the widower may come across as very sincere. However, you need to be extremely cautious about letting a widower back into your life following a breakup.

Most of the time when widowers ask for a second chance, it's because they're lonely, want sex, and miss the fact that you cleaned the house, cooked the meals, and helped out with the kids. It's *not* because they have any intention of opening their hearts or realize that they made a mistake when they broke up with you. The *only* time you should consider giving widowers a second chance if they've resolved *all* the issues that caused the breakup in the first place. That means that he needs to show, not say, that he's ready to make you number one.

For example, if he refused to introduce you to friends and family, he should have a date and time when you're going to finally meet them. If he had a shrine to the late wife in his home, it needs to be gone. If his closets were full of the late wife's things, all her stuff needs to be given to family or a thrift store. Only if he's done all the heavy lifting should you consider giving him a second chance.

Even if the widower does everything you ask, you still need to decide if giving him a second chance is worth it. Showing his love for you isn't a one-time event. It's something he'll have to do day in and day out as long as you're together. In addition, there will still be widower issues that come up from time to time. Have an honest internal dialogue with yourself as to whether or not you want to deal with the unique situations that come with committing your heart to a widower. There's no right or wrong answer to this question. Trust your gut feelings and proceed with caution if you feel that a second chance is warranted.

If widowers say they'll make these changes *after* you get back together, don't believe them. They're not serious about opening their hearts. They're simply trying to win you over with sweet words. These widowers have no intention of making changes. They simply miss the companionship and hope they can seduce you back into a relationship that will never progress.

AVOID THE FRIENDSHIP TRAP

Instead of asking for a second chance, some widowers will suggest that the two of you should be friends. Your answer to the friend request should always be a resounding NO. Being "friends" won't help widowers open their hearts. When widowers say they want to be friends, what they're really saying is that they want a relationship of convenience—one where they dictate the terms of what you do and how often you get together. He's tempting you with the idea that there's a chance the two of you will reconnect once he doesn't have the pressure of a relationship, but that will never happen. When widowers ask you to be friends, what they're really asking is that you put your life on hold indefinitely.

When it comes to relationships, widowers need to be all in. All a friendship does is prolong a relationship that's not going anywhere. If a widower says he wants to be friends, tell him that if he wants to spend time with you, it has to be as his girlfriend, fiancée, or wife—not a friend. As was discussed earlier in this book, widowers have a gut instinct when a relationship is right. When they want to pursue the friendship option, they know deep down that the relationship will never become serious.

WHAT TO DO WHEN YOU END THE RELATIONSHIP WITH A WIDOWER

When women end relationships with widowers, it's usually because they're frustrated and fed up with the men's inability to move forward and open their hearts. They're tired of competing with ghosts, they feel like they're in second place, and they no longer have patience for the constant stream of widower-related issues that never seems to go away.

Whatever your reason for breaking things off, the best thing you can do for yourself when it's over is to walk away and never look back. This can be hard, especially when you think the widower is a great guy and you saw so much potential in the relationship. In the long run, moving on with your life is the best thing you can do for your emotional and physical health. While ignoring him and cutting off all contact probably won't make him change, it will send him a more powerful message than an email, text, or anything else.

After the breakup, don't waste time agonizing over how the widower is doing. Instead, focus on yourself. Hold your head up high and act like you don't care. Don't respond to his texts, phone calls, emails, or other messages. Better yet, block his phone number, stop following him on social media, delete his emails, and don't go to places where there's a chance you'll see him. Do what the widower never had the courage to do and move forward with your life.

Breakups are never easy, but they're the first step to finding someone who's ready to open his entire heart to you. You deserve someone who will treat you like a queen—someone who's going to slay dragons, walk a thousand miles barefoot over shards of glass, or swim across the ocean just to be with you. You deserve someone who won't let the past stand in the way of his future. Go out and find that person.

It's the best thing you can do for the widower and yourself.

KEESHA'S STORY

I consider myself a mentally healthy, self-aware individual who did a lot of internal work to heal through counseling and coaching prior to meeting my widower. I knew the rules of dating and was pretty good at it. I didn't have low self-esteem, and I was successful and confident.

A friend I had known for twenty-plus years asked me out. He'd been widowed for a year. He was handsome, physically fit, successful, and would do anything for me—at first.

Because he was such a great guy/catch, we dated for thirteen months. I saw immediate red flags. All he could talk about was his late wife. We had several talks in the beginning, and I let him share how he felt about her death. I was compassionate, but it started to consume the relationship.

After watching Abel's YouTube videos, I brought up areas of concern like him calling her his "wife," pictures in the house, and posting on social media. I told him I'd rather him heal fully than date. He was already in counseling and convinced me he was ready. The pictures were removed, he started referring to her by her first name, and after a while, he shared his stories only with friends, family, and his counselor. I decided to commit.

After a few months, things changed. He pulled away, and his interest and effort were minimal. I got frustrated. He lashed out toward me, and it became *very* toxic. I should've left. However, I let the years I've known him and who I thought him to be cloud my judgment. I also tried to change him, which was wrong. Once he showed me who he was, I should've left.

He experienced widowers' guilt and felt bad about dating me. He didn't vocalize this until a time when I was ready to leave. He also was a torchbearer. Every time I'd walk away and call it quits, he'd reel me in with tears and promises to change, and for a short time, he would. I also noticed that when someone else died in his life or he experienced work/life stress, he'd regress. The emotional and sometimes verbal abuse (being overly critical, getting smart, being mean or curt) would start—and the devaluing. He displayed frequent Jekyll-and-Hyde type behavior, causing weekly arguments out of thin air and frequently accusing me of being out to get him, even though I was the only consistent support he had.

I learned that he wanted me to take the wife's place physically. He often discussed marriage, even though initially, I wasn't interested. He wasn't a liar, and I believe he meant it, but he had no intention of investing in me as a person or the relationship. He only wanted a wife to fill the void. During the relationship, I met family, friends, and coworkers, and I was never a secret. But he couldn't let go of the past. He was angry that I wasn't his late wife.

I woke up one day, and I had lost myself. This self-aware, confident woman allowed him to pull her into feeling sorry for him and being a constant supply of empathy and support, all while none of my needs were being met. I was invisible. I'd bring these issues up, and sometimes he'd change. Toward the end, he expected the benefits of having a wife without putting in the work to get one, and he wanted me to ignore my own needs, which wasn't an option. It became clear to me that I was there only for his benefit, so I blocked him from *everything* and haven't looked back.

He asked me to stay. I told him I did myself a huge disservice and wasn't loving or honoring myself properly, and that I refused to continue settling. I was so focused on what I wanted that I couldn't focus on what was really happening.

It's been three months post breakup. I've remained single and refused to talk to men while I heal. I spoke with my life coach, friends, and family; became reconnected with myself, my passions, my needs, and my loved ones; and dealt with the part of me that clearly felt I deserved less on some level. I binge-watched Abel's videos and other self-growth content. I had a great foundation to start, so I was able to get back to me. I'm proud to say I'm fully back!

ANDREA'S STORY

I dated a widower four years after his wife passed at the age of thirty-four from a long fight with brain cancer. His late wife and I worked together, and it was her family that introduced us. I did not know him prior to her passing other than the fabulous stories I heard about what a great guy he was during her illness. I proceeded into this relationship cautiously, as this would be new dating territory for me. I had never been married, nor had children of my own, and had never dated a widower. How different could it really be?

The relationship progressed naturally, and before long, I was in a serious relationship with a widower, his kids, his family, all the torchbearers, the ghost of his late wife, and the late wife's entire family. I assumed that because he was young, had a whole life ahead of him, and his late wife's family had introduced us that he must be ready to love again. I was correct except for the fact that his late wife's family *did not* want him to move on with his life. It appeared that way on the surface, but in actuality, they were in full control of him, his kids, and our relationship. I unfortunately did not figure this out until it was spiraling out of control. I found out too late that there were no healthy boundaries set by the widower for his late wife's family and his kids.

When we initially started dating, his home was a shrine to his late wife. It did not bother me at first because I knew he had two young daughters and she was their mother. They were ages seven and five when their mother passed away. The widower eventually felt it was time to remove many of his late wife's pictures. After about six months of dating, he did so with the exception of a few kept in his kids' rooms. We communicated about the pictures being put away after he took them down. He told me it was time, and that he loved me and wanted me to feel comfortable in his home. I thought we were all moving in the right direction until the late wife's family walked into his house and noticed the changes. They became enraged that he did this without their *permission*. To appease them, the widower put everything back.

I found myself "celebrating" the widower's wedding anniversary—initiated by his late wife's sister (the same one who had introduced us). We also were expected to "celebrate" the late wife's birthday for an entire month. The problem was that none of these events were "celebrations"—they were all-out mourn fests set in place by her sister to keep his kids and the widower in a miserable and depressed state of mind. He expressed to me that these "celebrations" were not healthy, but that he would continue to go with the flow to please everyone. I learned quickly that you must have a different kind of confidence when dating a widower. You must be willing to understand that there are many facets to this complicated relationship, but it is not impossible if the widower is strong enough to set healthy boundaries prior to dating and not take the "please everyone" approach.

I ended the madness after one year of dating and us trying therapy together. I could no longer paint the red flags white and realized I was settling for a life built around him, not us. I accepted that the widower was not ready to date and not strong enough to set healthy boundaries. He came back after six months, and we tried again, but nothing changed. As a matter of fact, it was worse.

Now here we are, three years later. He recently contacted me, asking for another chance at us. I let the widower know that it took me a long time, but that I came to peace with it all and have moved on with my life. I have maintained mutual friendships who tell me that not much has changed, and that his life continues to be manipulated by his eldest daughter and the late wife's family.

I, on the other hand, have realized that you should not surrender your love to someone so laden with grief and guilt. In my opinion, these are the reasons he felt compelled to acquiesce to his late wife's family. The red flags were blazing, and it became clear to me that in spite of the love I thought we shared, this was not the place for me to be happy.

11

MARRYING A WIDOWER

I PROPOSED TO JULIANNA THIRTEEN months after Krista died. When I got down on my knee and asked Julianna to be my wife, I knew I could happily spend the rest of my life with her. There was, however, a small part of me that worried Julianna would say no. I knew she loved me, and over the last couple of months, we had talked at length about getting married and making our lives one. Still, I wondered if she had overcome all of her widower-related worries and concerns. Did she really want to spend forever with someone who would always have a small part of his heart reserved for another woman?

After we became exclusive, Julianna informed me that she wasn't going to play second fiddle to Krista and would only marry me if she was certain I was ready to open my heart and start a new life with her. Over the seven months we dated, I had done everything I could through actions and words to let her know she occupied the top place in my heart.

Would it be enough?

When I got down on the snow-covered ground and popped the question, the biggest smile I'd ever seen burst across Julianna's face. I knew her answer before she said anything.

"Yes! Yes! Of course, I will!" she exclaimed. Then she threw her arms around me, and we tumbled in the snow together, kissing, smiling, laughing, and crying all at the same time.

Two-and-a-half months later, we were married.

As I write this, it's been sixteen years since we exchanged vows. During that span, we've had seven kids, moved four times, and had more ups and downs than we can count. We've experienced days when we've been blessed with more than enough and other days when we barely had enough to make ends meet. Life has been one unpredictable adventure after another. Yet no matter what unexpected direction life has taken, we've made each other and our marriage our top priority.

And, yes, there have been occasional widower-related setbacks. I've mistakenly called Julianna by Krista's name at least a dozen times, teared up when an impromptu memory of Krista flashed through my mind, and had bursts of anger over Krista's suicide. Most of these moments occurred early in our marriage, but when they happen, we've worked through them and refocused on each other. Because of that, our relationship is stronger today than it was when we exchanged vows sixteen years ago. Julianna is the love of my life, and every morning I wake up grateful and happy she's the one by my side.

Some say that a marriage to a widower must be a relationship of three hearts, with the new woman and the late wife each getting an equal share.

I strongly disagree.

A successful marriage to a widower requires just two hearts: yours and his. While the widower will always love the late wife, for a marriage to last, it has to be your heart and his beating in unison. Feelings for the late wife have to be put in a special place, or you're always going to feel like you're competing with a ghost. If you feel like you're in second place, there's no way the relationship is going to last. Don't deceive yourself into thinking things will improve *after* you get married, because they won't. If he's not treating you like a queen now, he won't be able to do it after you tie the knot. If a widower asks you to marry him, there should be no doubt in your mind that he's ready to move on with you. If you have concerns or worry that he's not ready to take this step, trust your gut. It's better to delay marriage until you're sure he's ready to make you number one than to live a life together knowing that he'll never love or care about you as much as his late wife.

Julianna is the primary person in my life and the center of my universe. But don't take my word for it. Julianna can explain in her own words what the last sixteen years have been like.

JULIANNA'S STORY

I still remember the moment when Abel dropped the widower bomb on me. We were in the middle of dinner on our first date. After I learned he was a widower, I wanted to run from the restaurant where we were eating and never see him again. Dating a widower was something I had never considered. I was twenty-three at the time and really didn't want to date someone who had been previously married, let alone someone whose wife had died just six months earlier.

The rest of the evening was a disaster, as we were unable to talk to each other. After Abel dropped me off at my apartment, I drove to my parents' house and told them about the horrible date. When I told them I never wanted to see Abel again, my dad said Abel deserved a second chance.

I was stunned. A second chance? Was he serious? Did he really want me dating someone who had just lost his wife? Didn't he think there was someone better out there for me?

So when Abel asked me out a second time, I said "Yes," but I told myself this was the last date the two of us would ever go on. That second date was followed by a third, fourth, and fifth date. Each date got a little bit better, and soon, we were spending practically every day with each other. It wasn't long before I fell in love with Abel. But could I marry him knowing that he'd always love Krista? I wasn't sure.

I realized I had to make a decision. It wasn't fair to either of us to continue a relationship if I couldn't accept Abel's past. I either had to move forward with Abel, or end things. I thought long and hard about the decision. In the end, I chose to commit my heart to Abel. My love for him was only part of the decision. Abel worked hard to make me the center of his universe. He wasn't perfect at it, but I felt that our relationship was always moving toward marriage—something we both wanted. On the day he surprised me with a wedding proposal, I couldn't help but say "Yes!" I knew he was the man I wanted to spend the rest of my life with.

Our sixteen years together haven't been perfect. Like all couples, we've had our good days and our bad ones. But even during the hard times, I've always known that Abel loves me and accepts me for who I am. I also know that I occupy the top place in his heart. I don't worry about competing with a ghost because that rivalry isn't there. Our marriage is the two of us moving forward together and putting each other first.

Marrying a widower wasn't something I ever thought about until I met Abel. Looking back, I realize that dating a widower was a blessing in disguise. It forced us both to decide what we wanted from a relationship, then make the necessary sacrifices and commitments to ensure we were each other's number one. That hasn't stopped widower issues from arising on occasion, but we've worked through the issues together, and our marriage has been stronger as a result.

I love Abel with all my heart. I'm looking forward spending the rest of this life and the next one together.

BOOKS

BY ABEL

RELATIONSHIP GUIDES

Dating a Widower: Starting a Relationship with a Man Who's Starting Over

Marrying a Widower: What You Need to Know Before Tying the Knot

Life with a Widower: Overcoming Unique Challenges and Creating a Fulfilling Relationship

MEMOIR

Room for Two

NOVELS

The Third

The Time Seller

ABEL KEOGH is a relationship coach and the expert on widower relationships. A remarried widower, Abel has successfully helped thousands of women know if the widowers they're dating are ready for a serious relationship. He also helps widowers understand what it takes to overcome grief and open their heart to another woman.

Abel is the author of four books on widower relationships and a memoir about losing his late wife to suicide and falling in love again in the year following her death. His "Dating a Widower" YouTube channel contains valuable advice for widowers and the women who are dating or married to them.

Abel is also an avid runner. He and his wife, Julianna, live in the beautiful state of Utah, and as citizens of the Beehive state are parents of the requisite seven children.

To learn more about Abel or to schedule a coaching session, visit http://www.abelkeogh.com.

REFERENCES

1 Jane E. Brody "When a Spouse Dies, Resilience Can Be Uneven," *New York Times,* September 26, 2016 https://www.nytimes.com/2016/09/27/well/family/when-a-spouse-dies-resilience-can-be-uneven.html

2 Hannah Furness "Men more likely to die after losing their wife, but women carry on as normal" *The Telegraph,* October 22, 2012 https://www.telegraph.co.uk/news/health/elder/9625818/Men-more-likely-to-die-after-losing-their-wife-but-women-carry-on-as-normal.html

3 Emily Yoffe "Hollywood's Widower Fantasy," *New York Times,* August 8, 1993 https://www.nytimes.com/1993/08/08/opinion/hollywood-s-widower-fantasy.html

4 Debrah Hecker "Relationship Success: Balancing Togetherness and Individuality" *Huffington Post,* February 13, 2014 https://www.huffpost.com/entry/relationship-success-bala_b_4776478

5 Psychalive "The Importance of Self-Worth" *Psychalive,* https://www.psychalive.org/self-worth/

Printed in Great Britain
by Amazon